For Rocky -

Bardo Stations

by

E.J. Gold

Gateways

Text and content © 2005 by E.J. Gold
Graphics from video games of the same names © 1986-2005 GODD Team: E.J. Gold, Barbara Haynes, Richard D. Hart, Claude Needham, used with permission
Screen shots © 2005 E.J. Gold, Barbara Haynes
Cover photographs © 1987 E.J. Gold
Cover design Marvette Kort
Typesetting Tabatha Jones
Layout Avikagrafik, using the Times New Roman font, the choice of author E.J. Gold, and his science fiction editor and writer father, Horace L. Gold
Proofing Tabatha Jones

Published by:
Gateways Books and Tapes
Post Office Box 370
Nevada City, California 95959-0370
800.869.0658 • 530.272.0180
gatewaysbooksandtapes.com

Printed in the USA

Gold, E. J.
Bardo stations : bardo training manual for the pre-deceased / by E.J. Gold.— 1st ed.
p. cm.
Summary: "A self-help reference book for the Afterlife. Describes one hundred thirty-one Bardo Stations to assist the Afterlife Voyager in selecting rebirth — an accurate method of intentional reincarnation"—Provided by publisher. Includes bibliographical references and index. ISBN 0-89556-178-6 (pbk.)
1. Future life. 2. Death. 3. Reincarnation. I. Title.
BF1311.F8G645 2005
133.9'01'3—dc22

2005023183

Bardo Stations

Bardo Training Manual for the Pre-Deceased

by

E.J. Gold

First Law of Recurrence:
"Lessons Unlearned Will
Be Repeated"

Gateways Books and Tapes
Nevada City, California

E.J. Gold

Table of Contents

INTRODUCTION

When I first began working on the Bardo Stations, we had no virtual reality; videogame technology was not yet in its infancy, so I wrote about them, and set up HO Scale tabletop photography using a pinhole lens on a Canon AE-1 35mm camera. These color shots together with text and sound effects were published as a CD-Rom under the title "BardoTown" available on the web at idhhb.com.

Then, some 20 years ago, the technology that I had been predicting for over 45 years came along. We formed a Game Development Team consisting of Dick Hart as our Chief (and only) Engine Programmer, Claude Needham as our Text, Sound and Weapons Designer; Barbara Haynes as our Levels Checker — she repairs the wrong textures, broken spawning points and tweaked walls, ceilings and floors that remain after I have spent 20 hours juggling math calculations and weaving my way through the primary Level design.

Our G.O.D.D.™ First-Person 3-D Open GL Fogger Engine was scratch-built by Dick Hart; having tried building in virtually every other engine available, I can tell you that it is among the best gaming engines ever built. It can do anything the major release engines can do, but it was designed specifically for me to use for the purpose of making Bardo Levels for Bardo Training; it was never intended for entertainment, and therefore does not utilize the bang-up whirligig whizzing camera rotations or extreme violence and wild pyrotechnics of the typical gaming engine, although it could do those things if we wanted to make it do them.

I have at my disposal over 10,000 sound effects and music tracks, and the same number of wall, ceiling, floor and environmental textures. I can record whatever I want to and put it into the engine. It will accept my strange requirements for spaces and creatures to put into them, and I can design my own 3-D models and place them in the system.

Because of the visual 3-D illusion and the phantom surround-sound which utilizes only two speakers, the effect of Full-Immersion is created for the user. The addition of multi-million colors and the screen detailing which came with Open GL makes the illusion even more profound.

You will believe that you are actually in the Bardo, and that shock of recognition is precisely the idea.

As you work through these Bardo Spaces in the virtual reality of the Bardo Training, you will find that they will affect you, and penetrate into your Daily Life. You will experience moments when you can see that your everyday activities are reflections of Bardo Voyaging, and your dreams will definitely become more vivid as your Bardo Experience is transferred back and forth between the conscious and unconscious mind.

Lucid Dreaming, which we call NightWalking, is a direct result of Bardo Training, and it is in these vivid dreams that your Bardo Experiences are permanently recorded. One specific effort of the Bardo Training is to bring those experiences into the conscious mind and to give the Voyager some volition in the Voyaging Experience.

This book attempts to familiarize the reader with some of the Bardo Stations of the Between-Lives State. They are suggestive of the Bardo Training Experience, but they are not the Bardo Training Experience. They lack the vivid color, 3-Dimensional effect, self-directed movement and interaction, sound and other qualities of the Immersive Experience of Bardo Training. Nevertheless, they may well induce Lucid Dreams in the reader.

The biggest shock of all to most readers is that what they have always considered their own private dreams are not at all subjective — that they are shared by all Bardo Voyagers, and that virtually everyone on Earth has been there, too.

The Bardo Station Workbook, available on the web at idhhb.com, is a companion book to the present volume which provides additional material for your personal Bardo Voyage here at the Bardo Training Center.

Both books together provide an introduction to, and virtual map of, the Afterlife, together with strategies for Voyaging toward a Higher Conscious Rebirth. It is my hope that you will use these tools for transformation for your efforts on behalf of all beings everywhere.

Yours in The Work,

ej gold

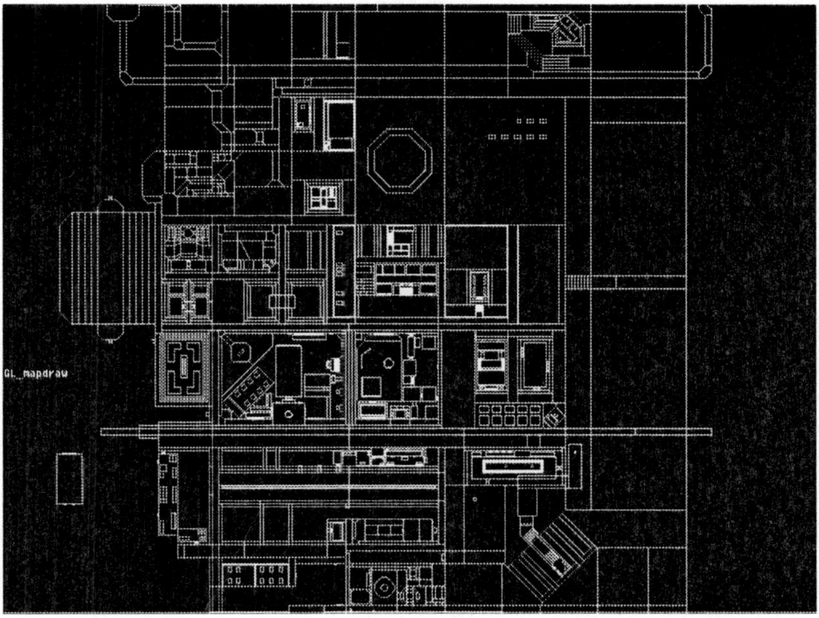

BARDOTOWN MAP

"This is station KGOD, Number One on your dial, coming to you from the heart of BardoTown. KGOD, the only station you can listen to... just try to turn us off." And that's just one of the surprises in store for you in the Rebirth Stations of the Third Bardo ...

You'll howl with laughter at the antics of the Black Gang; you'll scream with delight at the DownTown Clowns, and you'll gag with wonder at the growling wolfpack just behind you. Was that the gurgle of water, or your own suppressed giggle???

Here's the map you'll need if you're wandering in the Afterlife once again, in the Between-Lives State just before Rebirth. You can find maps like this in any BardoTown gas station, gift shop or boutique, but by the time you've figured out where you are, you're somewhere else.

Notes:

MORTUARY

One wakes up on a slab of concrete floating in air, somewhere in a dank basement. There is a door on the far side of the room.

Going through the door, one rises from the basement into a casket placed in the Slumber Room, a large front room within a small family-run mortuary on the second floor of a tenement building. One can see the street outside through the curtained window. There is a stained glass figure of a dragon behind the casket, and flower arrangements are placed on either side of the lectern.

The front door seems to be locked. However, there is another door leading out of the Slumber Room, through which one can easily pass into a heavily carpeted hallway with side rooms, in which are caskets on display. There are flowers everywhere, and doors which may open into mortician areas where bodies are prepared and arranged for funeral services. Soft music is playing throughout the funerary area.

The carpeting is thick and plush; there is a copy of the *American Book of the Dead* on a table to the left in the Slumber Room. One can also see a small lantern on a corner table.

Although all the ways out of the Slumber Room seem to be closed, a momentary consultation with Uncle Fred, who is in one of the caskets in one of the Viewing Rooms will result in the Opening of the Way.

Somewhere in the depths of the Mortuary, one will find the key necessary to pass through the locked front door.

There are other areas to be explored. Within the Cold Room one will find a tiny doorway which leads beyond the Mortuary into the AfterWorld.

The Cemetery holds some clues, and passing through the Final Gate one will be free of the body and its confines, and thus able to pass downward into the Blackout Stage of the First Bardo.

Notes:

ATLANTIS

Atlantis represents the passage of the soul into the very deepest, darkest depths of consciousness, the watery grave from which there is no return.

One finds oneself in a seemingly endless maze of riveted metal corridors, punctuated with heavy bolted hatchway doors and airlocks, set in a powerfully constructed bulkhead structure, under billions of tons of water, which is feelable and oppressive in the pressure of its unguessable weight overhead.

One threads one's way through the metal corridors, clanking on the iron-topped ramps and stairways, ever-downward into the lowest levels of the Undersea Kingdom, until one finds oneself in an enormous domed area, within which one will find an array of prismatic ceramic Soul Houses similar to those made by the ancient Babylonians and Egyptians to place in the tombs of the departed, which is you.

Suddenly, without warning, cracks begin to develop in the dome. There is a sound of widespread panic; the sound of the dome splintering and the roar of water filling the void is overwhelming as your silver escape capsule slowly rises to the surface of the water.

Notes:

WHARFTOWN

Upon arriving at the surface of the water, one finds oneself on a wharf which serves as a street in a canal zone of low roughly-made buildings. There are several such streets connected to one another, threading their way through a series of canals below.

A small two-story building stands out from the rest; it is called "Jenny's Place". You will want to enter there and seek help. You may have to find your way through a maze, and help may not always be obvious; things are not always what they seem.

Notes:

CARNIVAL

The First Carnival lives up to the meaning of the word "Carnival", meaning a Celebration of the Flesh; it is a meat-oriented Lower Bardo Space, with pleasure-driven attractions and seductions everywhere, and the sound of the sea not far away.

There are screams of thrill-seekers on the Giant Rollercoaster, and fun-seekers ride the carousel, dance away the hours, shoot at moving targets and a big fat growling bear in the shooting gallery, throw coins at plates and rings at bottles and try to win the big teddy bear at the concessions.

The Big Top has three rings, clowns abound, and the rides through GhostTown and VampireVille attract long lines of eager passengers.

Notes:

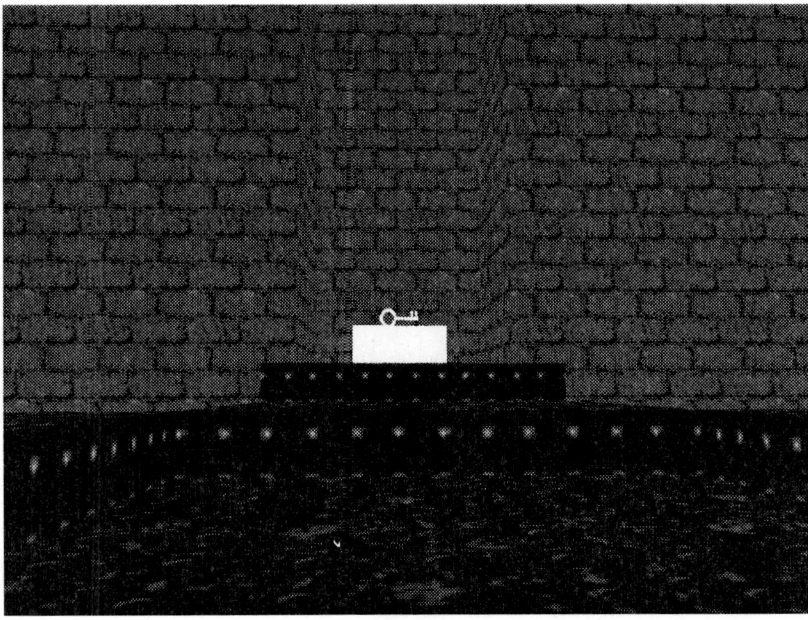

ARCADE

The Arcade's main attractions seem to be glamorous shops and glittering, attractive merchandise. Tucked cunningly and unobtrusively amongst them you may find the Bardo Training Center, where you can learn to pass through the Bardos into a higher rebirth. Row upon row of chairs placed before gaming computers are arrayed within.

Notes:

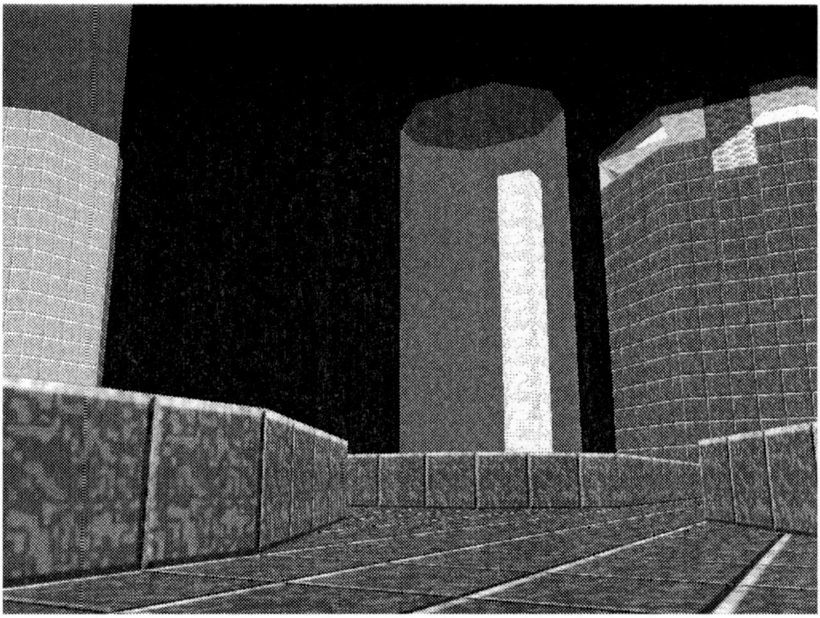

BOARDWALK

The Boardwalk leads past the Carnival, into a small beach town, where yet more seductions await the unwary Voyager.

One encounters the BedSheet Hospital here, and eventually one may find the Fun House at the end of the Carnival's Cacophonous Midway.

Notes:

FUN HOUSE

One finds oneself in an old-fashioned walk-through Fun House. The exhibits are murky and the corridors are dark, dank and uncomfortably narrow, stinking of adrenaline and old urine; the odor of cooking hot dogs, popcorn, cotton candy, roasted peanuts and ribs is laced with the more delicate aromas of ice cream and flavored snow-cones. Everything is sticky from being handled by candy-covered sweaty hands, and the floor is covered with discarded bubble gum, prophylactics and other less identifiable substances.

Laughter rocks and rumbles in the distance, and the threat of sadistic and terrifying creatures is as oppressive as the humid heat which is not dissipated by the slow passage of fan-driven stale and salty air.

Ghosts and goblins appear and vanish; the tunnel seems endless and the corridors twist and turn in labyrinthine patterns as one wends one's way through this nightmarish scene.

Finally, the exit appears before one, and the door opens to allow passage into the next station.

Notes:

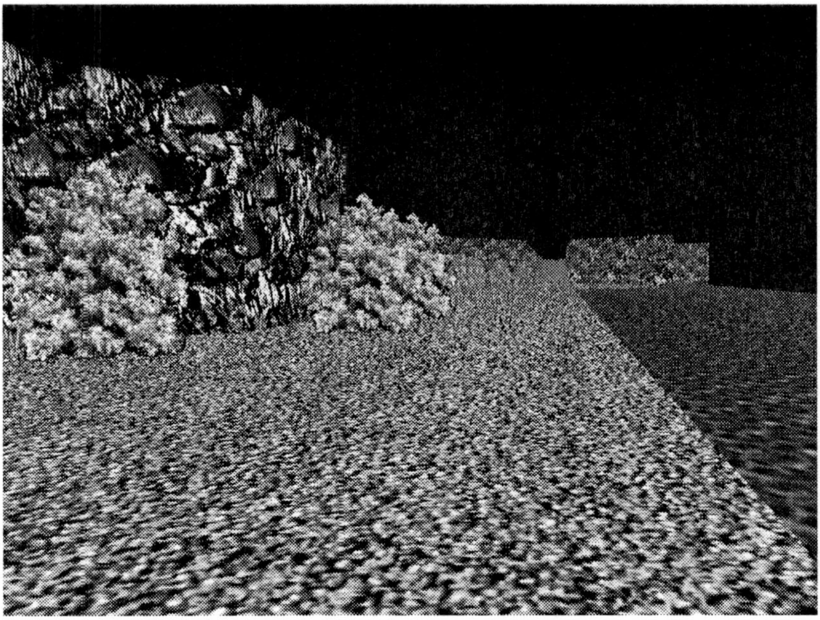

PACIFICA

In a cold light drizzle of icy rain, one finds oneself on a long, lonely road, leading through endless forests, low cliffs and ravines to an equally lonely rocky cliff, below which is an equally empty beach, to the west of which is an endless ocean of cold, still, clear water. There are no vehicles on the road, no other travelers, no one in the small hamlets and villages which one passes on the way to somewhere, but exactly what the destination might be is very unclear. At the end, there is only darkness.

Notes:

PARTY HOUSE

One finds oneself in a lighthouse on a dark and lonely beach. Nearby there is a rather large two-story country house, within which a party seems to be ongoing. No one responds to you, however, and the party is obviously one of those that never stops, that just goes on day after day, night after night.

There seems to be no way out of this Party House, but if you persist, there might be an exit.

Notes:

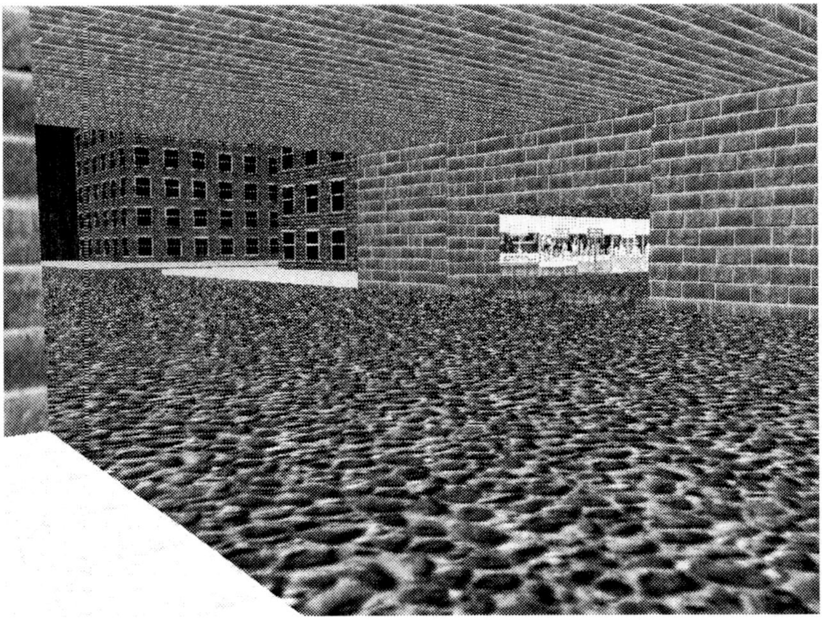

DOWNTOWN

At first glance, it seems just like an ordinary downtown area — high buildings, industrial section, shoppers here and there, lots of red brick and concrete.

It is here that you can find the Magic Talisman of Flying, the Cape of Invisibility and the Amulet of Post-Mortem Power, but there are dangers throughout this area, and the Black Gang is everywhere around you, ahead of you and notably, visibly and audibly behind you.

Notes:

OPERA HOUSE

One finds oneself in a small underground vault or mausoleum below a grassy park-like setting outside an enormous white stucco-walled Grand Opera House, which is encircled by a long driveway.

Within the Opera House is a magnificent lobby. Upstairs are the Rest Rooms, but it is doubtful that they offer any real rest. One is able to move through the entire Opera House, upstairs and down, in the balcony area, loge and even the basements where stage items are stored.

The aroma of sweet florals and the overwhelming smell of gardenias is everywhere; it looks and feels more like a marble-walled country club than a theater. There are traps everywhere, and the Phantom of the Opera is not only here, but he is definitely aware of your presence in his domain.

Notes:

PLAZA

An enormous compound consisting of dozens of reception counters in a large high-ceilinged airport ticket counter-style lobby; lawns and walkways outside leading to the wide super-highway are visible through very high glass windowpanes.

Many labyrinthine corridors open out from the main lobby, leading to strange and dark areas. There are travel consultants, room reservation counters and many hotel wallphones everywhere.

You will find a very large restaurant near the lobby, as well as a Main Room Theater, another theater in the back of the hotel, a myriad of meeting rooms and many boutique-style shops; there are hundreds of hotel rooms and suites in the 60 story hotel behind and above the single-story lobby which sticks out from the hotel proper into the lawned approach.

Car rental counters are on the right; there are several garages and repair shops in that direction. A most unusual bakery is outside the hotel to the left as one enters, as well as an equally unusual pottery shop featuring three pottery wheels. Several concrete buildings lie in that direction as well, but if you get caught in them, they will not remind you of anything remotely related to a resort or vacation spot.

In some of those hotel rooms you will find virtually everyone you know, doing just about anything you can think of that people do in hotels. There is no way out, but there are dozens of ways in.

Notes:

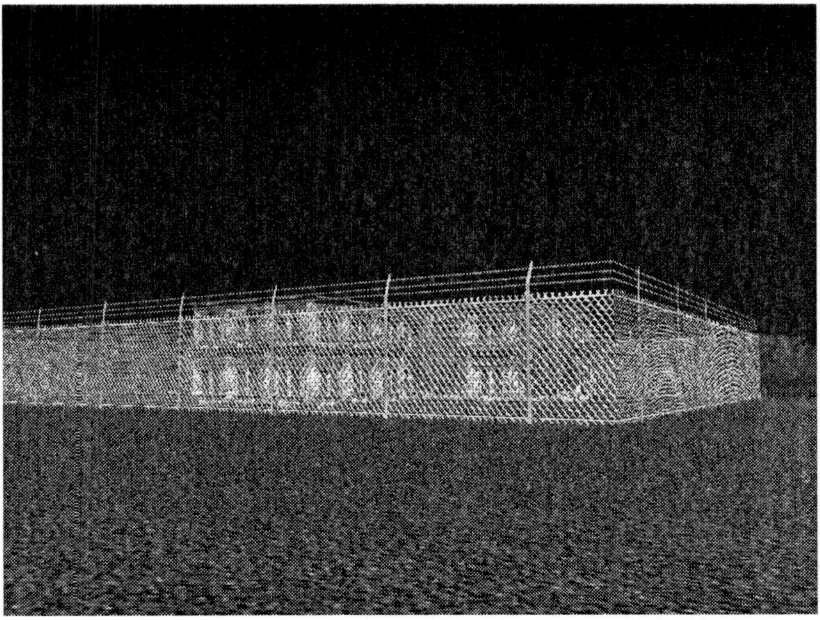

ASYLUM

Just to the West of the Plaza you will encounter a large Insane Asylum, called "Amazing Grace Home for the Criminally Bewildered". It is a place of endless corridors, elevators and open and closed wards. There are hundreds of beds, an equal number of bedpans and bars on every window. This is not a place to spend leisure time. If you manage to get out of here, it will not be wise to escape, but to sign yourself out; otherwise you will certainly be followed and recaptured and placed back here to remain incarcerated until you rot or the place decomposes, whichever comes first.

You will find Strange and Unusual DisOrderlies on the Violent Ward, zombies and ghouls in control of the Administration Offices — and Brain Moles — which will attempt to suck energy from you should you encounter them unawares.

Fear of cold and wet snakes could influence you to stay well away from certain areas. You will find a transporter in Room 255 and a silver chalice in the right hand of Jesus can be found in the Visitors' Chapel on the fourth floor. The Chalice gives extra life and energy, which might be needed in the lower dungeon-like levels of the Asylum, should you manage to stumble into them on your way out.

The Electro-Shock Therapy Unit delivers some 50 billion electron-volts of solid alternating current; if touched, it will result in total paralysis for oh, say, 6 or 7 minutes or so.

You will find John F. Kennedy in a rocking chair on the fifth floor, if you accidentally end up in the Extremely Disturbed Ward, along with Napoleon, who smiles as he runs through the wall.

Cleopatra and Caesar will ask endless questions, but answer none of yours; Sigmund Freud is too wrapped-up in his own problems to be of any help to you, and Joan of Arc has Alfred Adler pinned to a couch in the Atrium.

Carl Jung counts dead insects for you, if you have a need to know how many there are, and offers dried bones and fake treasures to passers-by such as yourself.

Pavlov will condition you for rebirth using bells and dog saliva unless you can get to the itch powder first and annihilate all the bats in the chamber.

Adolf Hitler, Mussolini and Atilla the Hun can be found in the shower rooms downstairs. They are not typically much help in negotiating the next turn, but can be persuaded to bring the stuffed nurse to the tiny frogs and blue rats in the kitchen.

Notes:

BOULEVARD

One finds oneself at the West end of a long, wide boulevard with a grassy island divider between the Eastbound and Westbound lanes.

Just less than one block down the Boulevard one will see an apartment complex outside of which is a large group of people, quite obviously dressed for a funeral.

One can go upstairs to the recently vacated apartment and view the corpse. You may or may not wish to look at its face.

Notes:

SUBURBS

You find yourself amidst row upon row of low single-story bungalows set among trees and grassy lawns; there is a small neighborhood theater nearby. It feels safe to walk here, but nothing could be further from the truth.

Narrow cement walkways are threaded between the rows of tiny houses. One can hear loudspeakers and announcements over bullhorns from just around the corner somewhere. They blare out orders to get off the street or report to the theater immediately.

A grassy knoll lies to the West of the Boulevard; the glare of brilliant street lights penetrates the area, and a harsh radiation of some kind that seems to be emanating from them can be distinctly felt, even without a material body.

The ground trembles with shock waves of low rumbling coming from somewhere below. Intense heat builds up as the morning turns into day, and a blistering hot wind rolls over the street. Everything seems to dim and waver into nothingness as you find your way to the fascinating two-story Beverly Hills style shopping mall just north of your spawning point.

Notes:

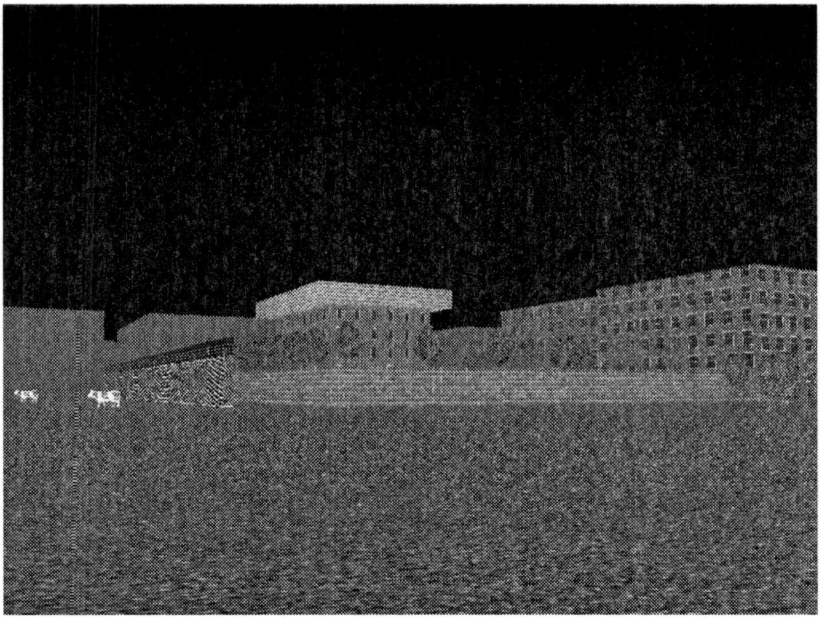

PARIS PARK

It is wartime, and nuclear weapons have been used, but this area has not yet received a direct hit. People used to walk these streets, but they are cold and dark and empty now, and the people are gone or in hiding.

Sirens sound and the cold wind struggles to thread its way through the concrete canyons; there is a small restaurant on a high mall, and the park beckons.

In the park, one finds a long stone stairway that leads downward to an enormous lawn. One can see a high chain-link fence stretching far into the distance, and cows on the other side of the fence seem to be grazing contentedly, seemingly unaware of the nuclear crisis all around them and unbothered by the additional Strontium-90 content in their cud.

Far in the distance you find yourself in some sort of compound, but its nature is not at all clear; is it a prison camp?

Yes, it is. The Prison Camp is surrounded by an electrified

chain-link fence; just beyond the entrance one can see small, low single-story barracks. One is apparently free to come and go, yet one can sense that this freedom is limited in some inexplicable way.

A long park-like path leads from the compound back to Paris Park. There seems to be no point to this, no event, nothing to accomplish, yet something prevents one from going on until the escape trigger is discovered.

Notes:

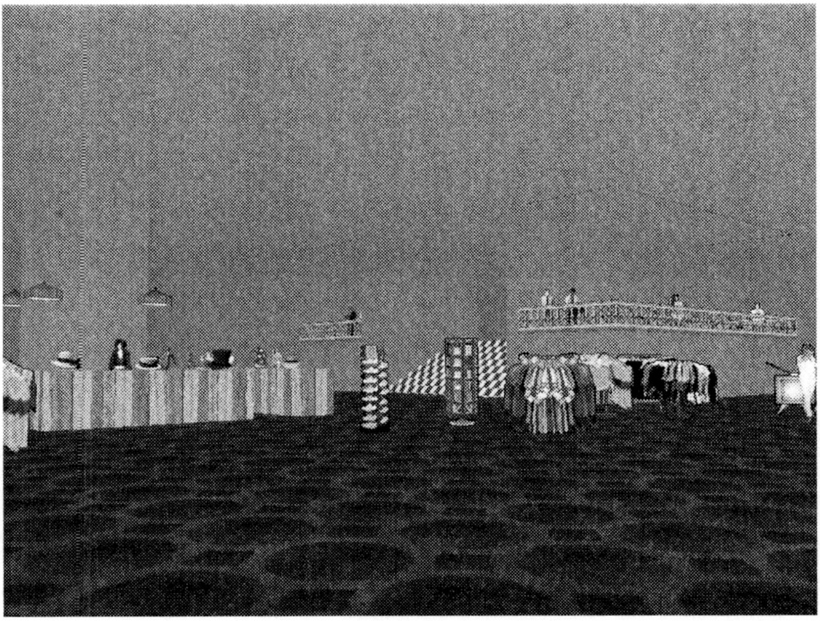

DEPARTMENT STORE

One finds oneself just outside a strange six-storied department store; on ground level there is a bus depot, within which many individuals are camped, apparently refugees from some enormous event.

Outside, on the street, one discovers a butcher shop and a dry cleaner's shop, one of which leads one into the department store's lower level.

There is an escalator in the depths of the department store, and it is to this device that one wends one's way.

At the top of the escalator, one finds several departments, one of which is the one for which you are looking.

Notes:

COLLEGE

The College is what we currently call a dormitory. On the second floor of the dorm, one will find the room one is looking for; jumping out the second-story window to save a few moments' walking time can be hazardous to one's rebirth.

Notes:

UNIVERSITY

The University consists of one gigantic building which houses halls of classrooms. One has the definite feeling of being followed, pursued by some unknown, and this sensation is quite justified. The boards have the answer for you, if you have the chalk to see it.

Notes:

PRISON FARM

One suddenly finds oneself standing in the middle of a Prison Farm. There are sentry towers and searchlights all around. Dogs howl and the moon is bright in the sky.

Notes:

BEACH HOTEL

One finds oneself in an elegant old hotel with large high-ceilinged corridors, fancy elevators and a grand ballroom.

Outside in the lush, verdant gardens, one can find celebrants in party formation, and along the corridors and in the darker service areas still more fun-seekers can be found having fun in a variety of ways, most or all of which lead to lower rebirth.

In fact, there is only one area in the Beach Hotel that does not lead to instant lower rebirth.

Notes:

VERANDAH HOUSE

One is led to the outside of a run-down two-story 19th century Antebellum mansion. It is completely covered in ivy and other vines. The second-story windows open out onto a wide gently-sloped rooftop, making it possible to climb down to the ground from there.

Within the house, various events are occurring; a card game is ongoing in the parlor, and some sort of political rally is ongoing in a large back meeting room. The air is gentle and a slight warm summer breeze wafts through the house.

Insects, mostly katydids and grasshoppers, abound, and their song is carried gently in the wind. There is an atmosphere of sleepiness and laziness, and one's movements seem lethargic and torpid. Somehow one is able to exit from a second-story window and descend to the grassy lawn below. There are flowers everywhere and the overwhelming smell of gardenias assails one with its heavy perfume scent.

Notes:

BARNYARD

One suddenly finds oneself across a yard from a low two-story farmhouse; there is a barn just on the other side of the grassy frontage, and a walkway between them, worn down through the years by tramping feet going to and returning from the barn.

The door to the farmhouse can only be reached by running past the giant six-foot tall four-legged chicken with teeth. Within the house one can find an entrance to the barn without crossing the yard.

A bull is out there somewhere, ready to chase and gore one. The stench of manure is potent and piquant. If one manages to reach the barn, one will find oneself on the ledge above the stalls; there is a strong magnetic pull that threatens to draw one down into the void on the other side of the ledge, and from which there is no escape once one has been pulled into the gravity well that is a black hole in the center of the barn.

There is another way, but it will lead toward a fence upon which the unwary can easily be impaled or crucified.

Notes:

OLD AGE HOME

The Old Age Home is just down the way from the barnyard; it is a building composed of four two-story sections made into a square. There seems to be no way in and no way out. Within the structure lies a balcony around the entire building, but none of the doors will open. One must find the way out before time runs out and the structure implodes into blackness.

Notes:

COUNTRY CLUB

The Old Age Home leads directly to the Country Club, a large golf course and single-story clubhouse within which one will find the means to continue on the journey, but here, sequence of events is of utmost importance.

The golf course is very expansive and hard to negotiate; there are sand traps, water traps and roughs and trees and, of course, greens.

The Club House is large; it contains a restaurant, bar, pro shop and nearby, a small number of cabins for visitors.

Notes:

MOUNTAIN VILLAGE

The Mountain Village is laid out alongside a mountain road that can only be reached by passing through the Country Club; the walk is long and the path is dull and dreary, the scenery relieved only by the occasional meadow between the endless treeline.

There are hundreds of inhabitants of the Mountain Village, who can be heard, but are never seen. There is a general store, a gas station, several bars, a restaurant, three real estate offices, a doctor, a dentist, a barbershop and, of course, a town drunk.

Notes:

MOUNTAIN GYM

Just past the Mountain Village one will come upon a Mountain Gym, an elaborate three-story building with basement, built down the hillside above a deep gorge which drops some three thousand feet into the valley below.

There is a sub-basement pool, a full gymnasium, several offices, guest rooms, a health food bar, a boxing ring, a wrestling pad, various exercise rooms, personal training areas and, of course, the inevitable locker rooms and showers. A pair of boxing gloves and a bar of soap may or may not help you to pass through to the next Rebirth Station, but without them, it might be impossible.

Notes:

ROUNDHOUSE

This is a place where once mighty railroad locomotives might have been stored and worked on by maintenance crews, but now it is empty and deserted; a cold wind blows in through the open doors, the tracks long rusted with neglect.

Deep within the Roundhouse one can see through the misty darkness the lights of glassed-in offices and narrow hallways running to the far side of the giant building between the office spaces. There is a cold dampness to this place, and a feeling of quietude that goes with long disuse — yet, somehow, it does not seem completely empty; there is a sense of watchfulness, and somewhere in the depths, a pair of yellowish, malevolent eyes glare out balefully in contempt and anger at one's intrusion.

Unfortunately for the unwary traveler, the only way out is through.

Notes:

DESERT ROAD

Along the long, quiet, dusty Desert Road, one will encounter only tumbleweeds, cactus, yucca trees and rocks, with one single exception: a single low building which seems to be a deserted gas station and general store.

There are two gas pumps in front of the building, and the whole effect is one of traveling backward in time to the late 1930s, when gasoline pumps like this still existed. Coyotes howl in the distance, and the wind whistles through the empty shop.

There is a service bay in the back, and several wooden barrels on the side of the building. One will find a water pump on the other side of the building, and several items are still on the countertop inside. The bathroom doors still open, but the stench inside is so powerful that it is impossible to remain in there for even a few moments without passing out cold, and that, of course, leads to instant rebirth.

At the far end of the Desert Road you'll come across a strange sight among strange sights — a long low white building with a red tile roof. On the West side of this, a stone amphitheatre. Seated there in many rows, five foot tall greenish telepathic slugs.

Within one part of the L-shaped building, a pottery which houses a Shaping Wheel upon which souls are shaped for re-birth.

Outside the building to the Northwest, many pits to house the Sleeping Souls.

To the South of this complex, a raging Volcano with lava pits all around; beyond this, many miles of desolation.

Far to the South lies BardoTown, to be explored in the latter part of the Third Bardo.

Notes:

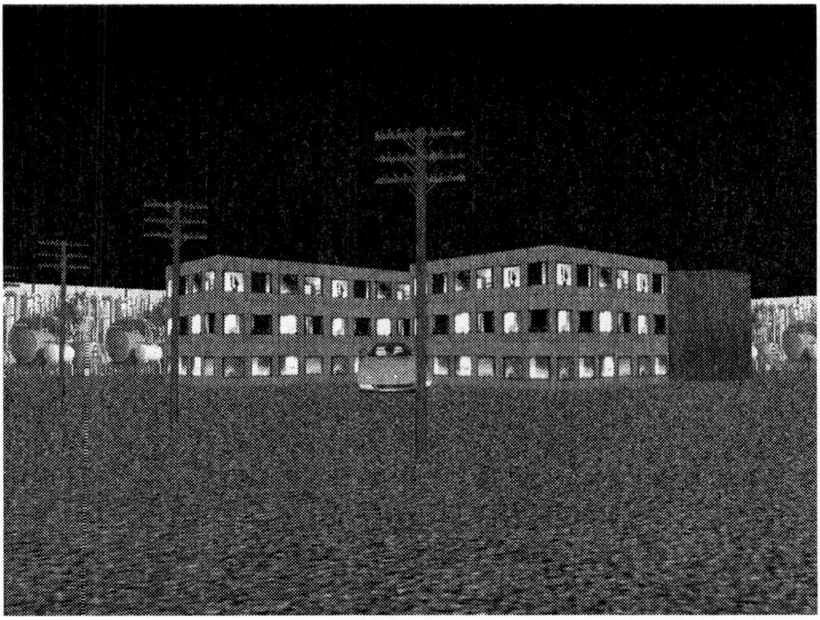

NUCLEAR PLANT

One finds oneself in the Eastern Mountain Range on a lonely red dirt road late at night. The sky is pitch black — there are no stars, and it is very cold. Blinking barricade lights signal the presence nearby of heavy construction equipment and imminent danger of some unknown kind.

Faint, eerie, threatening sounds of howling in the distance, of dogs, coyotes, wolves or something else not quite familiar, and no place to hide, nowhere to run.

At the end of the road, a gigantic Nuclear Plant. Sirens begin to sound as the Nuclear Core goes into the red zone; meltdown is not far away. Nobody else seems to be aware of the situation; it is up to you to find the Core Control Center and shut it down before it explodes.

Notes:

DIAMOND

Strange spaces abound here; you find yourself in a diamond-shaped environment in which absolutely nothing is familiar, yet you know you have been here many times before, perhaps in dreams.

Notes:

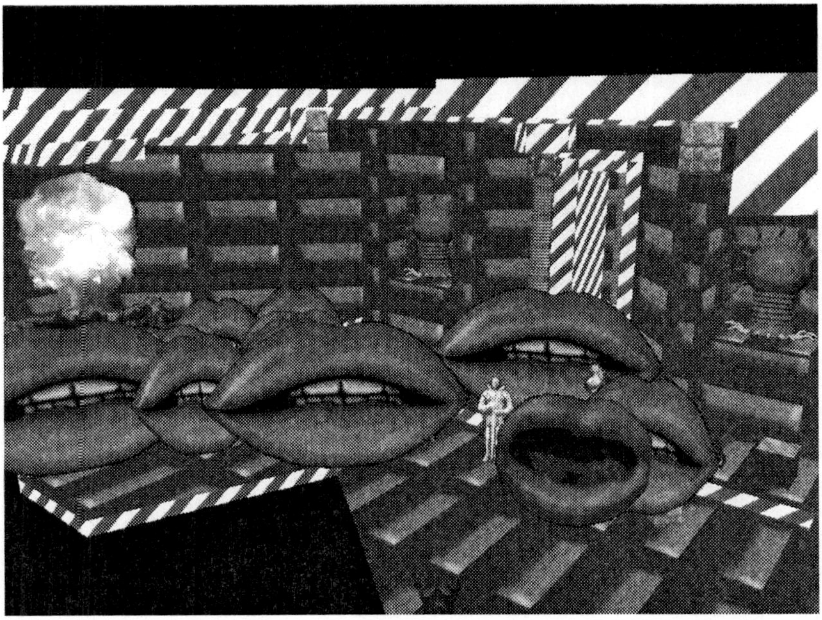

RHODAN

You are in something that might be the interior of a spaceship; the thought crosses your mind that you are not dead, that maybe you have been abducted by aliens, but as you explore the space, you realize that aliens would find this environment just as alien as you do.

There seems to be no way out, and even if you found a door, you know that empty space lies just on the other side of every outer wall.

The hum of unknown and unfamiliar machinery sends a chill through you as you explore the depths of this strange and unusual titanium-walled structure which seems almost alive; you are aware that it is conscious of your presence, and that it is somehow, in some occult way, directing your movements and responding to your explorations.

Notes:

UFO

Now you are sure that you have been abducted; this is definitely an alien space vessel in which you find yourself traveling through space at a velocity far in excess of the speed of light.

The aliens seem totally unaware of your presence, however; they take no interest in you and ignore you completely as you move about.

Stars are out there, but no constellations you have ever seen; then you realize that what look like stars are actually distant galaxies, that you are actually in deep space between groupings of stars, and that you are perhaps billions of light-years away from the nearest planet.

No thought of returning to Earth from this distance; you have come too far to even consider where your home galaxy, the Milky Way, might be.

Notes:

SCI FI

Not in space, not in time, not in any universe you have ever seen before, and you now realize that you have seen many.

Unfamiliar sounds, sights and a nightmarish quality to the environment in which you find yourself wandering, looking for something, not knowing quite what, but knowing that you are looking for something, and hoping that you recognize it when you see it.

Notes:

TECH 01

A technical achievement beyond anything on Earth lies before you and around you, but just exactly what it is and what it may mean is far from clear.

Gravity is nonexistent here, but then, so are you.

Notes:

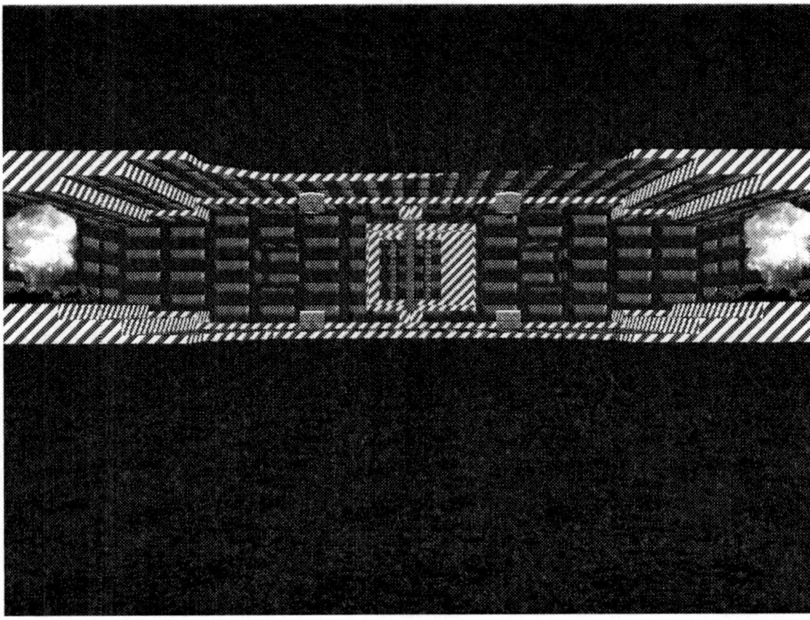

HERC 01

Is it a spaceship? Perhaps an alien world? Maybe something in the future? No, none of the above and, as you explore further, you realize that it is also none of the below.

Notes:

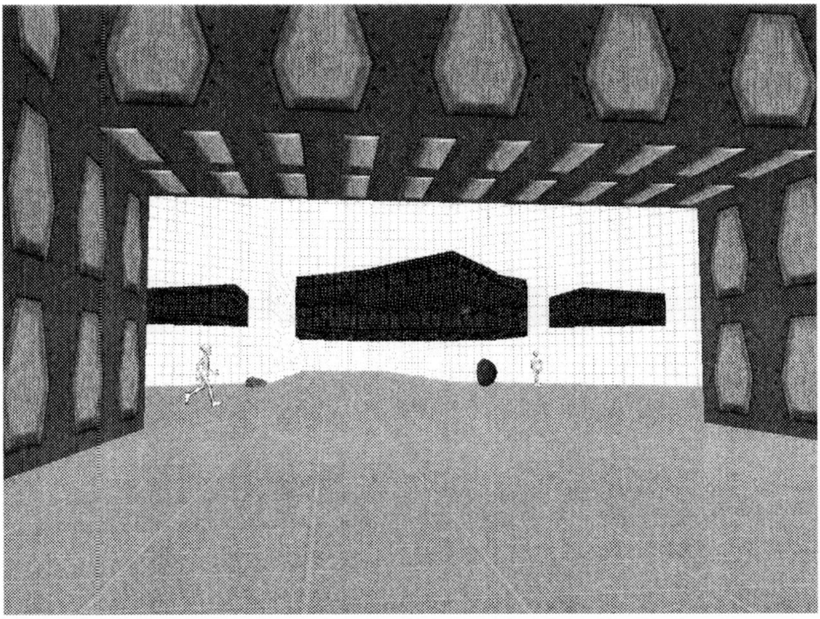

ROSTUN

You find yourself in a series of tunnels below a desert somewhere; there are aliens here, but they are not interested in you, and do not respond to you even when you attempt to question them or communicate with them. It is almost as if you were not here at all.

Notes:

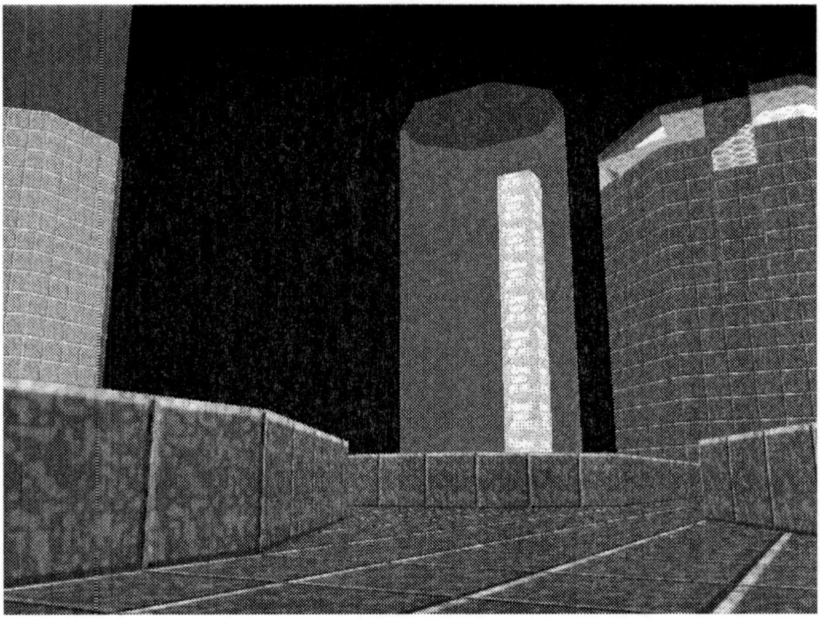

MARS CITY

The ancient capital of some red Mars-like planet; impossibly old buildings survive somehow in this alien landscape of dry canals and high buildings constructed of some material that seems to be impervious to the passage of time, just like yourself.

There are things to do here, places to go, but no people to see. Somewhere in this maze of strangeness there is a switch that will turn it all on, or turn it all off, or make something different happen, and that's where you're headed, in a wandering, roundabout way.

Notes:

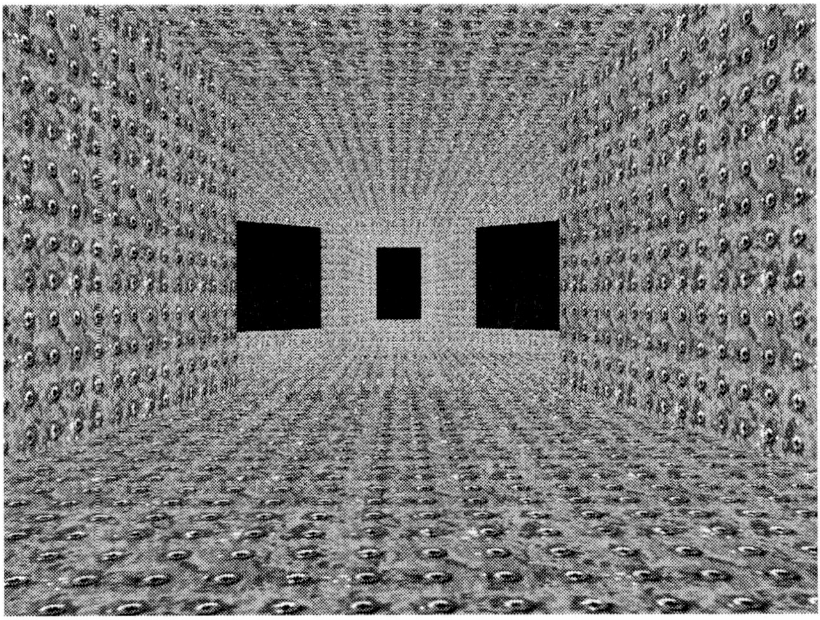

SPACE 01

Space is cold, space is silent, space is good. Without space, there is no time. Without time, all events would be in a single moment. Without space, everything would be just a single tiny blob, waiting for a Big Bang. You have no way of knowing just how long after the Big Bang this is, but at least the waiting for that Singularity is over.

There is nothing Out Here, nothing in particular to do. Just waiting. Waiting is.

Notes:

SOLARIA

You find yourself once again in Solaria, whatever that is.

Notes:

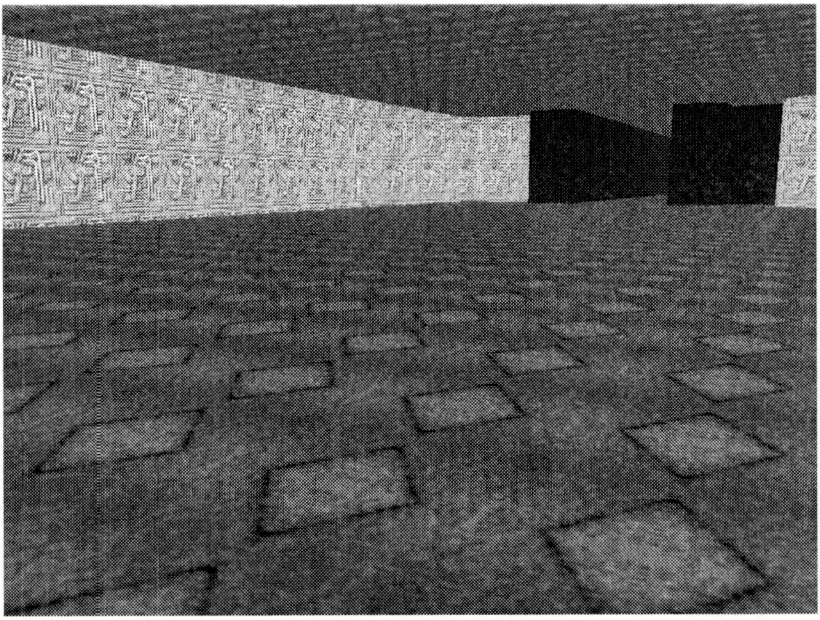

GREY

At last, an alien environment in which some aliens care about you and what you do. You are being watched, experimented upon and perhaps at some point, a few of your vital organs will be forcibly removed, or your precious bodily fluids will be extracted for some strange and bizarre purpose.

Maybe you are being kept for breeding, or as food, or even live bait for some horrifying monster that is waiting nearby to claim you and eat you alive, slowly, thoughtfully, chewing your best parts and spitting out the bones.

Maybe your brains are considered a delicacy by the creatures who have captured you; perhaps that book lying on the countertop nearby is a cookbook, and you're one of the ingredients.

Notes:

TUN WORLD

You find yourself in an endless world of endless tunnels and corridors, hallways and chambers, none of which make any sense or seem to have any purpose, just like you.

Notes:

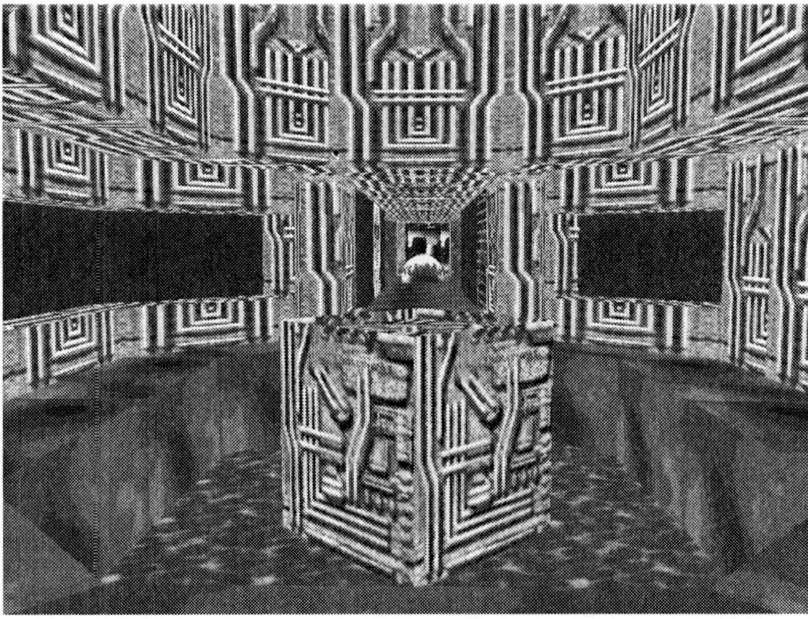

ABDUCTED

There is little doubt that you have been abducted, but by whom, or what?

And what, if anything, can you do about it?

Notes:

SLIME

Everything here is slimy and moldy and what isn't slimy or moldy is even worse.

Notes:

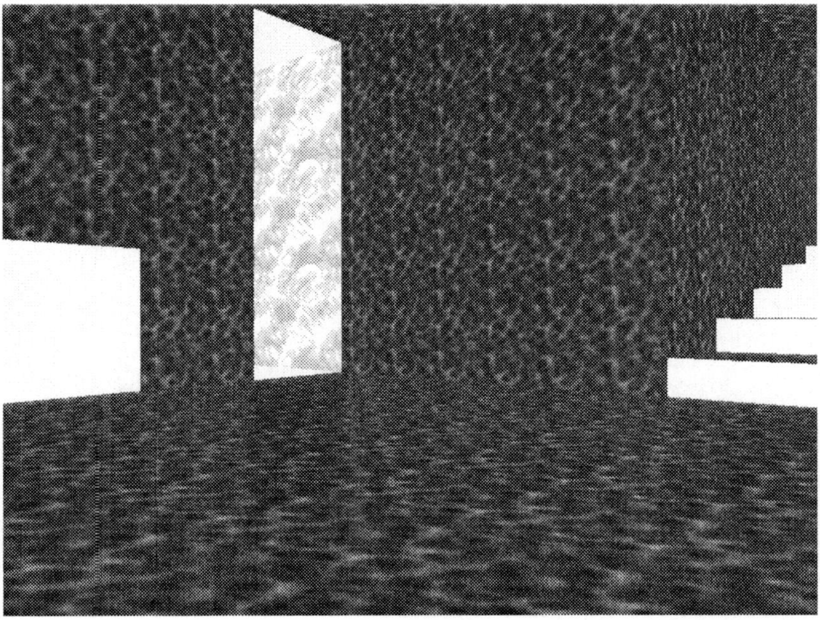

TREE OF LIFE

No mystic on Earth would ever guess that the Tree of Life is actually growing somewhere, but here it is, right before you.

Your job, of course, is to locate the watercan and give it a drink.

Notes:

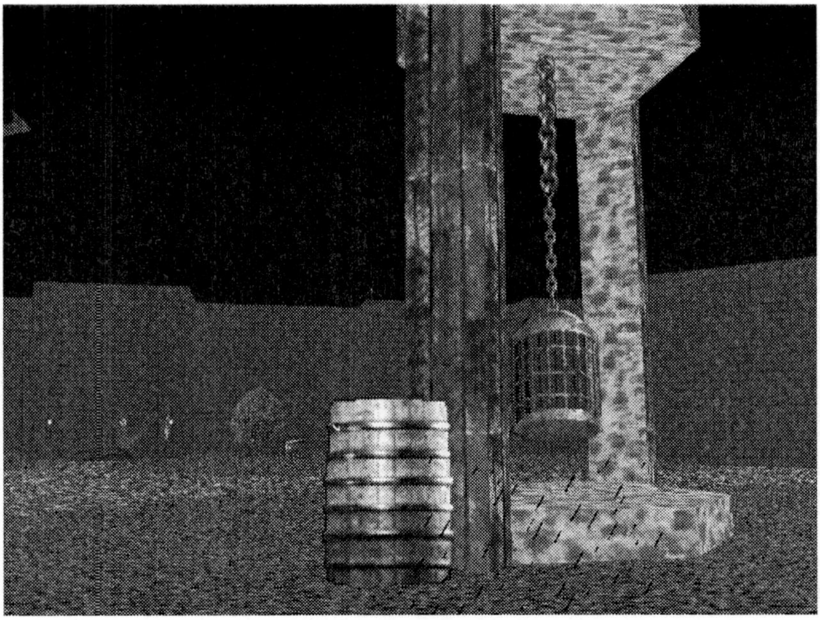

PAGAN

This is definitely not a space approved by any well-established religious group; hence, Pagan.

Notes:

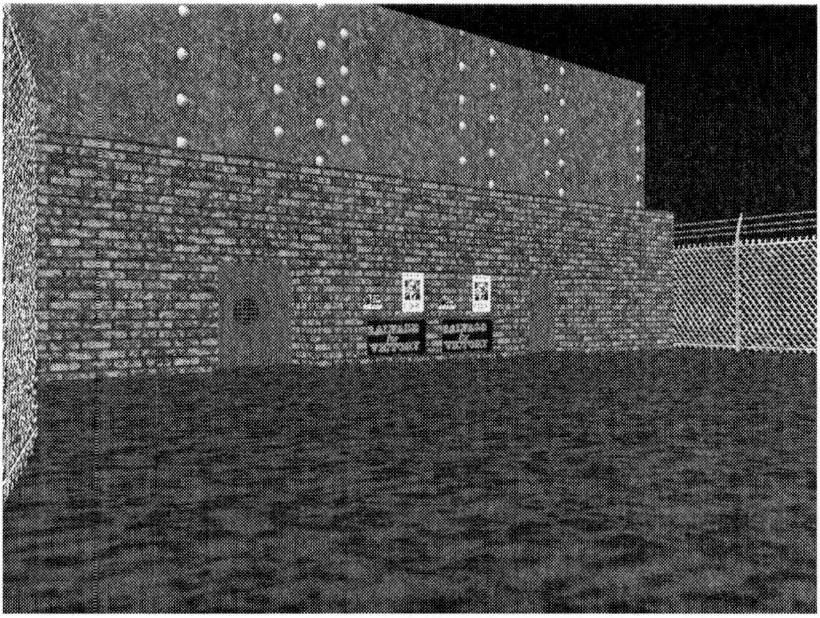

SHRINE

At the very heart of the Universe, the Shrine of Unknowing embraces you; somehow you know that you must not remain here, yet there seems to be nowhere else to go, nothing else to do. All time and space seem to be mere concepts here, nothing actualized, everything potential.

Notes:

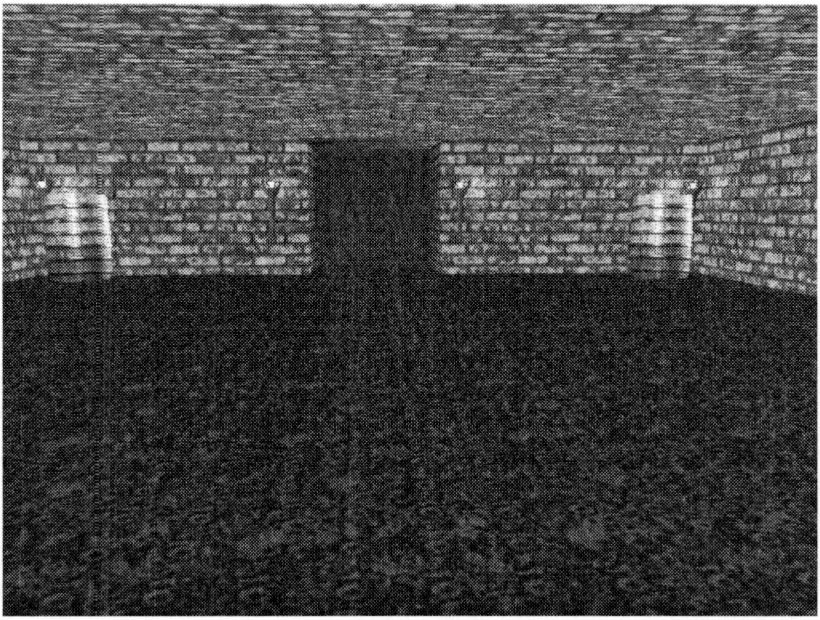

AARDVARK

Life sucks, then you die. It's at this point that you understand that nothing sucks like the Void.

Notes:

TOMBS

You find yourself in a long corridor, surrounded by tombs, mummies and stuff that a wide variety of creatures considered necessary for happiness in the Afterlife, including a video viewer and several loaves of French bread, wine and, of course, Thou.

Notes:

STONEHENGE

You find yourself in the midst of an open plain, surrounded by deep, endless forest. In the center of the plain, there is a group of gigantic stone monoliths, which somehow remind you of Stonehenge, yet the sky tells you that this is not Earth and that no human ever made or used these things.

Stars revolve at a rate that tells you that whatever planet you're on, it has a much shorter day than you've recently been used to. The rotation indicates a four-hour day if the rocky planet underneath you is about Earth-sized, some 8,000 miles in diameter.

Something tells you that within this enormous granite structure there awaits some mystical force that seems to draw you in, that wants you to walk into the center of itself.

Notes:

ZELDAR

You find yourself in the Mystical Kingdom of Zeldar; the Princess has been captured and lies languishing in a cell deep within the dungeons of the Evil Sorcerer Zaknar. Your job, of course, is to journey through this strange land and to find and rescue her. You feel compelled to carry out the quest and yet, it all seems so patently mythical that you have little hope that any of this is real.

Notes:

CASTLE DRAKE

You find yourself at the entrance to Castle Drake, whatever that is; yet you seem to know at least the name of the place. Just how this may be, you have no way of knowing. Deep within the depths of Castle Drake lies yet another dungeon, but this one is pleasant, familiar, dry and well-stocked with provisions along the way.

You also know that somewhere within this pleasant stone-walled palatial estate, you will encounter things that are not at all pleasant, and that the deeper levels of dungeon are far from familiar, dry and well-stocked with provisions. The squeal of rats tells you that it won't be long before the pleasantness wears off.

Notes:

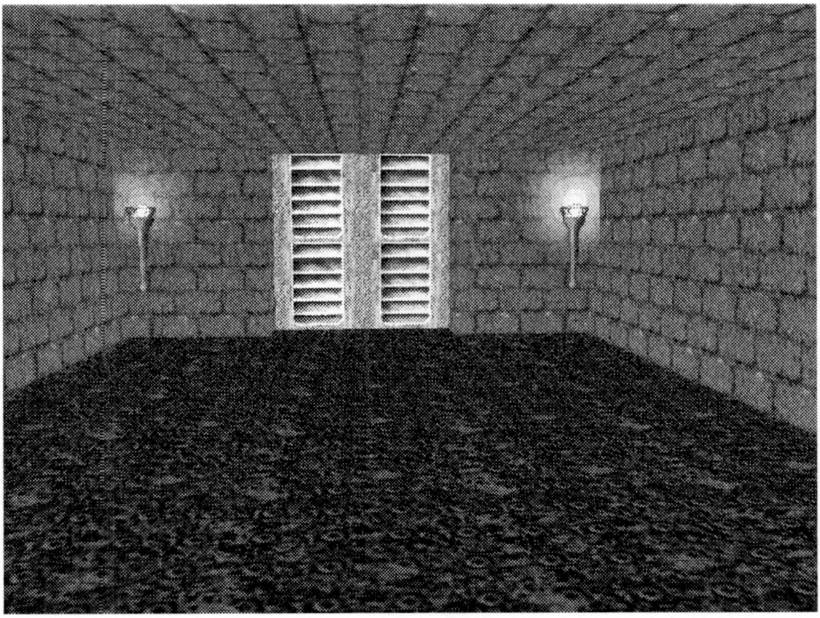

VAULT 01

You find yourself in the Vault of Castle Drake, but whatever happened above ground, you couldn't help ending up here. You keep telling yourself: It isn't your Vault.

Notes:

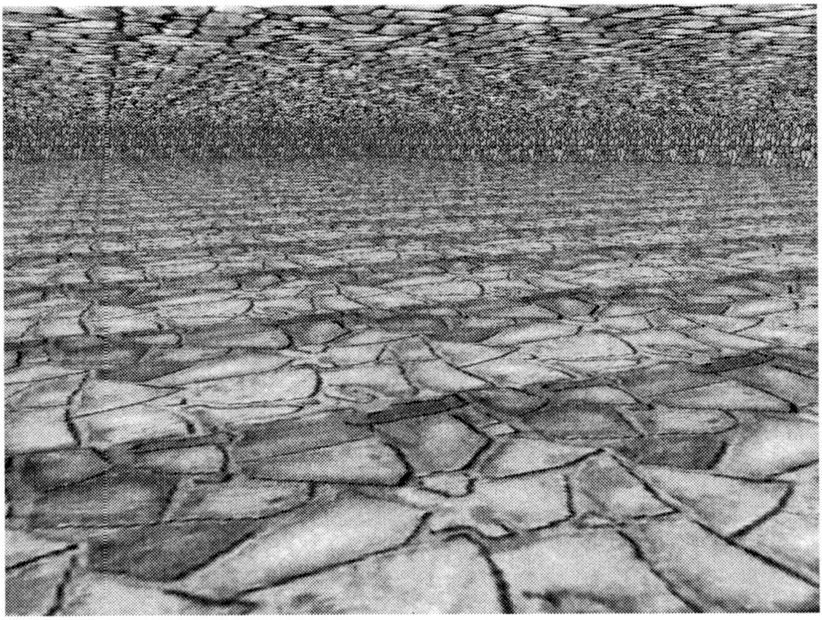

CRYPT

As if it hadn't already been creepy enough, you now find yourself in a slime-encrusted crypt, with dead bodies all around you. Clearly, things are going from bad to worse. If you happen to be a hungry ghoul, however, you're in luck. There are corpses in plentiful supply here.

Notes:

FORTRESS

At last, you find yourself in someplace totally safe; an impenetrable fortress surrounds you, with no windows, no doors, no way in and no way out; and what's more, you're completely, absolutely, totally alone in here. Or are you???

Notes:

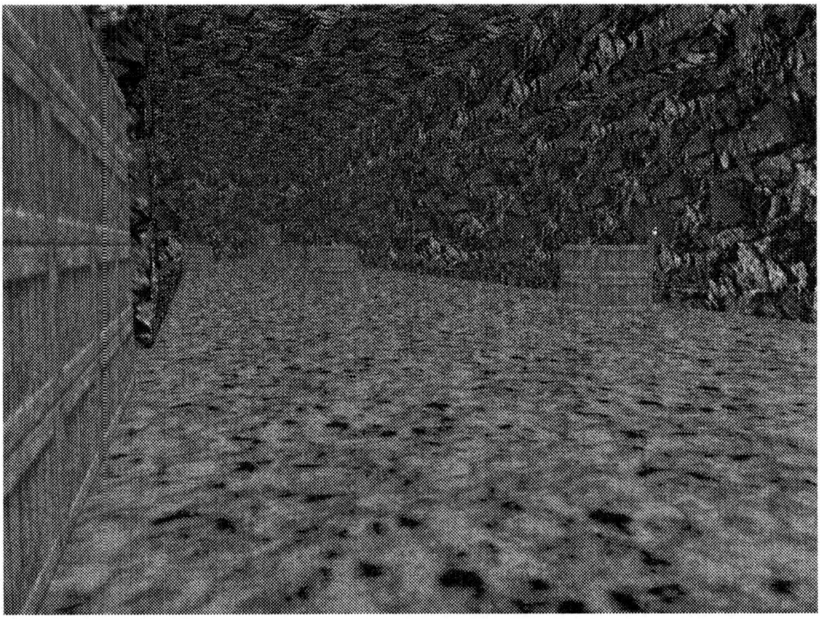

CATACOMBS

If the Crypt housed tons of dead bodies, the Catacombs makes it look virtually empty. Endless passages and labyrinthine tunnels make this an ideal meeting place for a Secret Society. Only problem is, how do you get Home from Here???

Notes:

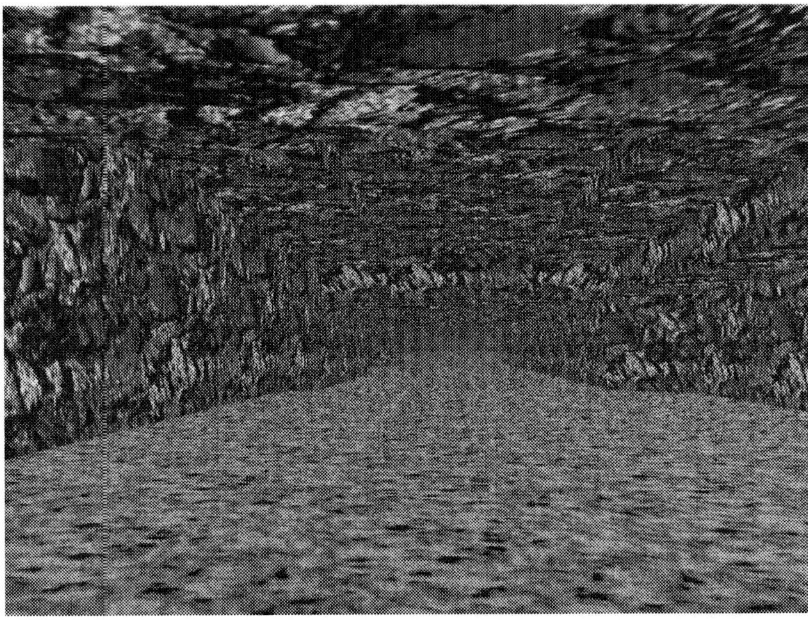

PLATO'S CAVE

Shadows on the walls tell you that you are in Plato's Cave. But where is Plato? You find yourself in a cave occupied by eternal beings who can never leave their individual cells. To communicate, they send etheric messengers—Avatars—of themselves, back and forth.

Linked telepathically, they also have a vision of the entire structure of The Cave as a single entity.

A jellyfish-like immortal creature in the very center of The Cave hangs suspended in gray featureless space, contunally flip-flopping into a variety of form-changes, each change representing one cycle of reality.

When it happens to see its other end, both ends writhe in revulsion; it screams silently in the soundless space at the center of The Cave, but there is no foreseeable end to its eternal suffering.

It has learned to fragment its consciousness, each fragment

temporarily compartmentalized into a smaller image of itself, and now resembles a gigantic geodesic honeycomb in which each separatized entity occupies one of its honeycomb cells, which results in what one now sees, The Cave.

Each of the fragments works toward ending the suffering of The One, the helpless Singularity in which they all have their ultimate existence.

The One cannot think of ways to end its suffering; all its energy and consciousness is absorbed by the continual unending Changes.

The separated entities are able to assume form, mind and sensations of The One in order to communicate with it what they have discovered and to report any progress toward a solution to the endless process of The Changes. They can now predict the procession of forms through their Book of Changes, the I-Ching. It is your task to find your way through this without becoming caught up in the Changes.

Notes:

MINE SHAFT

An endless maze of mineshafts and tunnels leads to the ultimate Mother of All Mother Lodes. You are about to discover the largest deposit of Heavy Metal anywhere in the Known Universe. In addition to the Heavy Metal, you'll also discover a plentiful supply of Swing and Hip-Hop.

Notes:

DUNGEONS

With all these dungeons, there must be a torture chamber somewhere...

Notes:

SEWERS

Dungeons were fine in comparison with this; sewers are meant to carry waste products out into some dumping ground, and these sewers are no exception. You can't help wondering if alligators in the sewers is merely a mythology, or if all those stories of missing sewer workers could have some basis in fact???

You hear a growling sound as you work your way toward some escape hatch, hoping to find some breathable atmosphere somewhere ahead.

Notes:

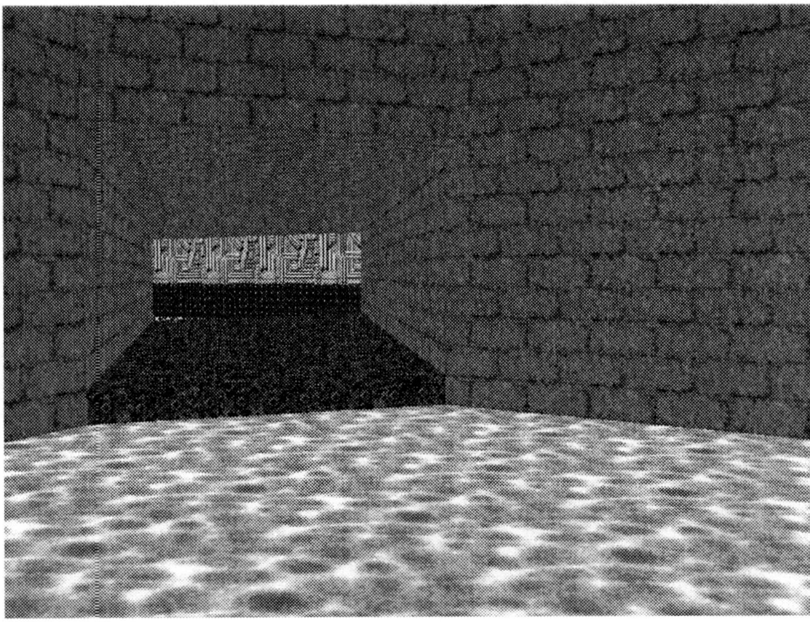

SATAN'S SHRINE

You find yourself in an endlessly descending spiral-shaped tunnel. There are Things along the way, and Stuff Happens to you as you wander downward.

Notes:

GOLDMINE

Gold, gold everywhere, but not an ounce to spend.

Notes:

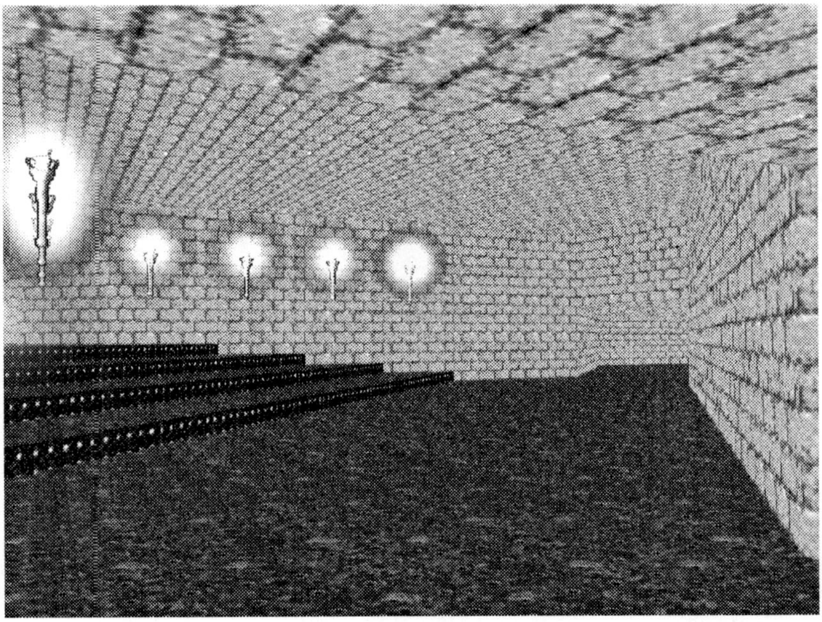

CURVE

The name says it all. A space-string that from outside looks like an endless piece of spaghetti, and from inside looks like there's bound to be something just around the next bend.

Notes:

CASTLE

If you were looking for a word to describe this stone-walled environment, "Castle" would come immediately to mind. One exception; nothing built this place, and no one has ever lived here.

Notes:

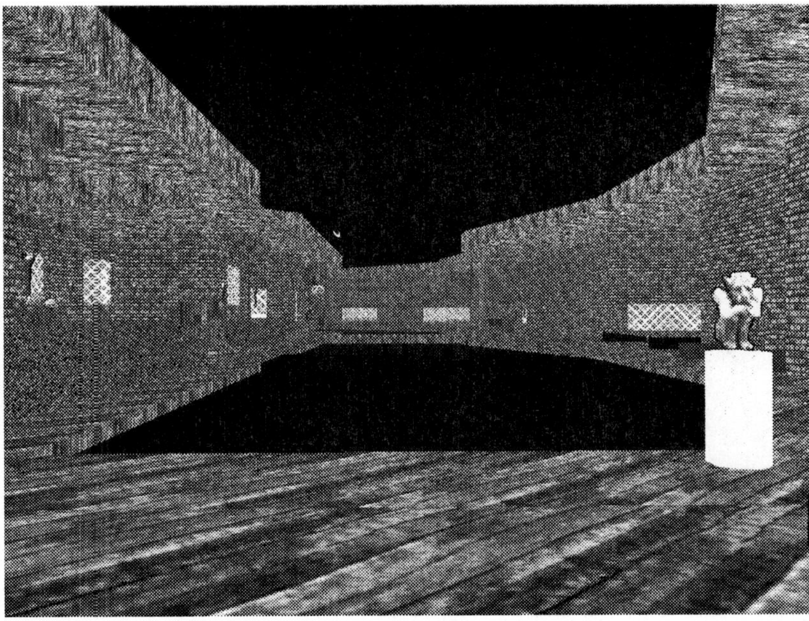

CARDIFF BY THE SEA

Ah, the salty smell and taste of the sea, the sound of waves crashing on the rocky shoreline, the feel of sand under one's feet, in one's hair and down one's back!

A cobblestoned street, a magician's lair, and an alchemist's shop await your inspection, and who knows where a ride on a rustic carousel might lead?

Over and under stone bridges and wooden stairways, some paths lead directly to the goal, but where are all the children, and what have they done to their eyes?

Notes:

TEMPLE

A Place of Worship, clearly, but of what, and by whom?

Notes:

CEMETERY

Beautiful crypts and mausoleums, greater and grander than any home for the living, people are dying to get in here. Truly magnificent designer tombs, homes of architectural grandeur, this is truly to die for. Pre-Need Plots aplenty. The sign out front reads, "Vacancy", and this means You.

Notes:

SHOJI

A simple zen environment with a tea ceremony just completed can mean only one thing — you missed a snack.

Notes:

WORLDCON

A World Convention without a convention; what a concept! With all these convention badges and hotel rooms, there must be a crowd of conventioneers around here somewhere. And where are the hookers?

Notes:

RAT RUN

Is it an enormous space, or are you just very tiny? Yes. One finds oneself in a gigantic space. Red and Blue spheres of light hang suspended just out of reach. Above them and below them are similar spheres on every level of existence.

It might be an enormous room, but the scale could be anything. It might very well be that you have found yourself in a dollhouse. An incredibly large eye looks through the window.

The eye observes the activity within.

Notes:

PISS POOL

If you've never had a bath or held a swim meet in a pool of piss, you're in for a treat.

Notes:

SKYWAY

A highway in the sky, this road leads to nowhere. Fast.

Notes:

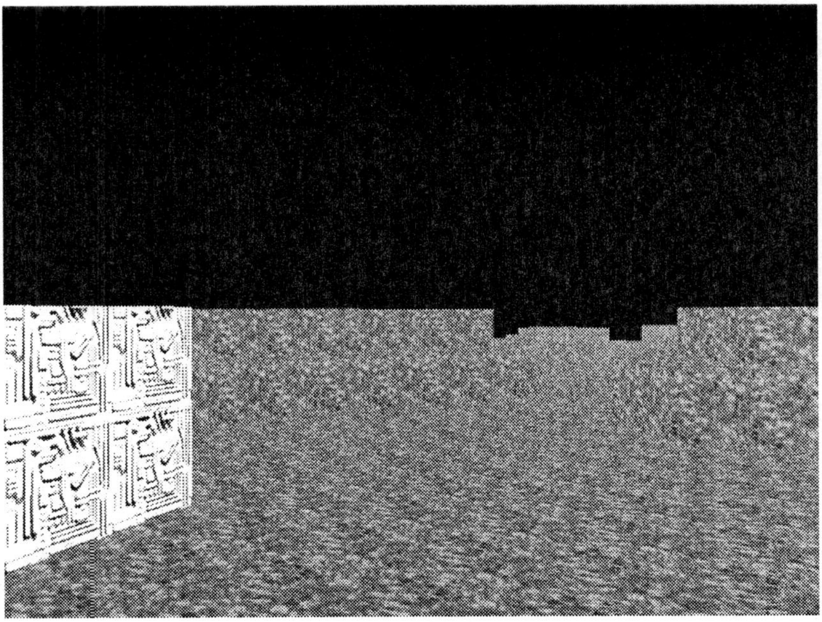

PEAK

You find yourself at Peak, and it has nothing to do with a mountain.

Notes:

THE LAST RESORT

This is the Last Resort, after which you'll never have to go to another one. See Paris and die? Not at all; die and see the Last Resort is more like it!

Notes:

BORDELLO

Bordello is just another word for whorehouse. Tired of Commercial Sex? Turn off the TV and just watch a movie and enjoy some Commercial-Free Sex!

Notes:

CON

Everyone who ever was anyone will be there at the Big Con. Not merely a convention, this is the high-school reunion of everyone who ever went to high school, grade school, kindergarten and university. You'll meet everyone you ever knew, if you can find anyone at all.

Don't know how to dress for it? Come As You Were.

Notes:

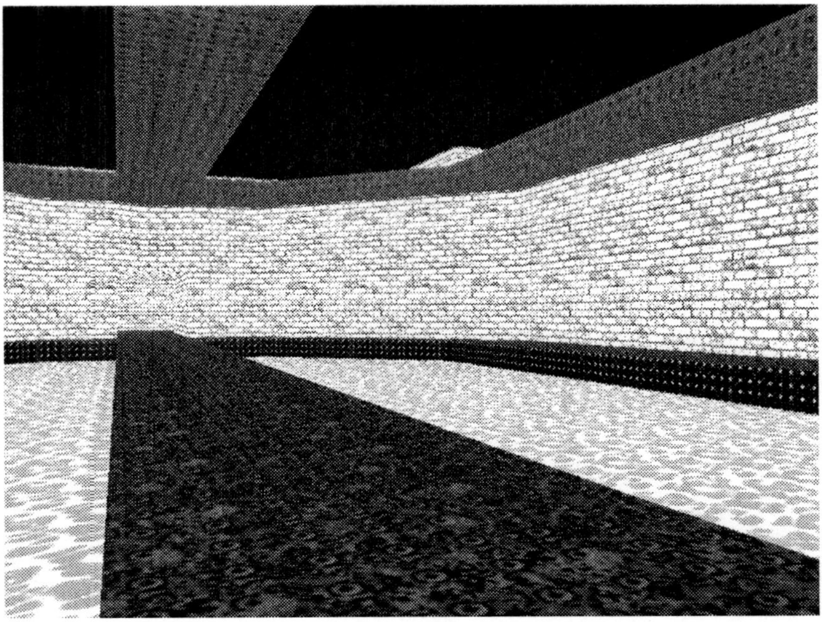

OVERPASS

Many rivers to cross? Try this bridge for a change of pace.

Notes:

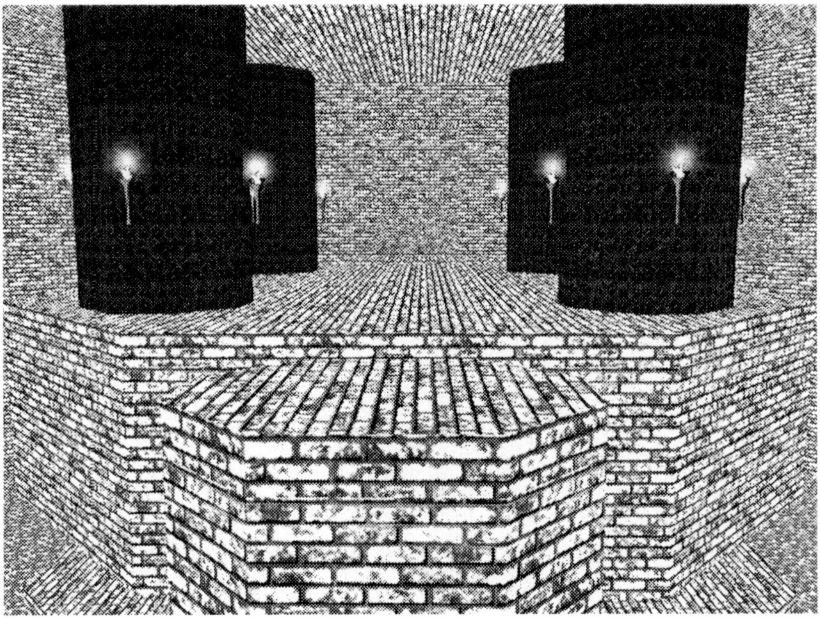

ROUND ROBIN

Here you will find nothing whatever, but it sure seems like something.

Notes:

FIBONACCI

The Fibonacci Series is the mathematical formula that describes the descending area of a spiral sea-shell, but that tells you nothing about what this space is all about; the best you can do is to grin and bear it.

Notes:

PENTHOUSE

You find yourself in a large penthouse; it reflects the tastes and trends of the very rich, and represents the continual urge to relieve boredom, but always it has within itself the seeds of its own destruction. As below, in the streets, so above, in the penthouse.

Notes:

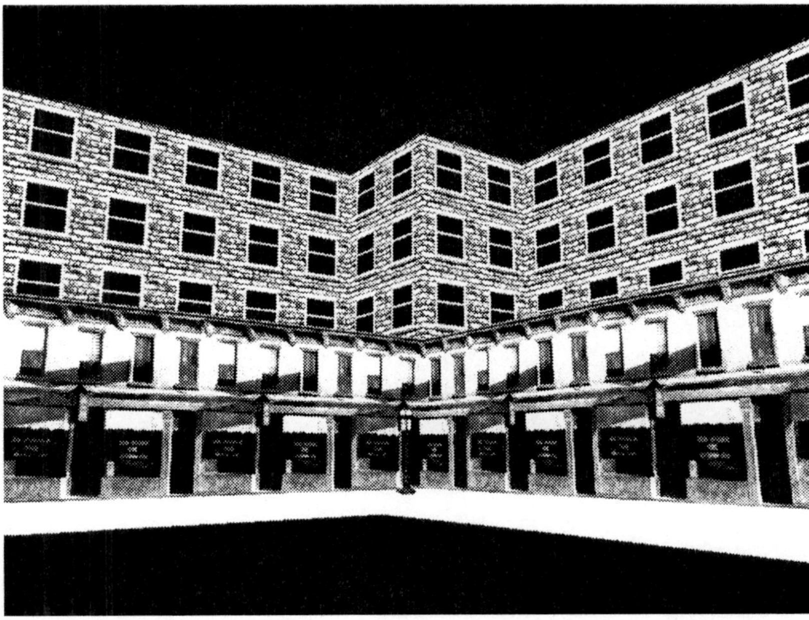

NUNAN

In the very depths of Despair, a small town near the California-Nevada border, one finds some respite from the continual fear of being hounded and driven by the Black Gang and packs of wild dogs. Now one is driven by Nothing Whatever.

Of what are most of us afraid? Why, Nothing Whatever. And judging by the sound of heavy breathing and stealthy footsteps, it seems to be getting closer and closer.

What's that, just behind you? Nothing Whatever.

Notes:

ONE

One is the loneliest number, and this number is no exception. When you're alone, you're all one, and as you've discovered before, it's very, very lonely at the top.

Notes:

CANNIBAL

One finds oneself on a small low-riding canal boat which slips past a low bridge near something that might be a theme park. The boat reaches harbor as night comes, and the lights of the city can be seen in the distance.

The distant screams might be people on a rollercoaster, but this is a cannibalistic society, and somehow you know that the screams are not people having fun, but being eaten alive.

The still water reflects the starlight, and the fear of victims and laughs of delight of the hunters echo in the otherwise silent air.

In this canal zone, you can only be one of two things; that which eats, and that which is eaten. If you're very, very lucky, you can escape both destinies, but you'll have to hurry. This sector is timed.

Notes:

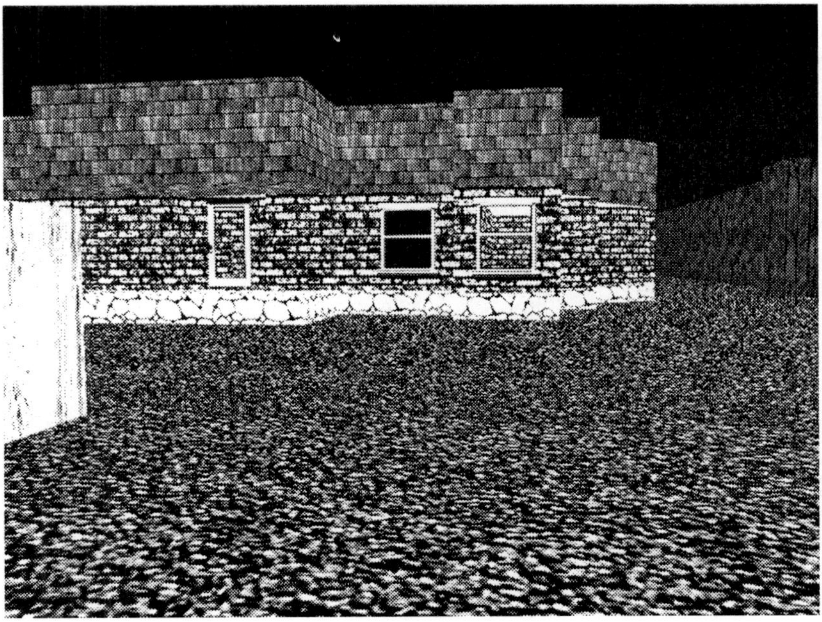

FARM

One finds oneself in front of a single-story New England farmhouse at the end of a long dirt road. There are a few small outbuildings on the property, and some farm implements can be seen here and there.

A large hen-house and other animal pens are evident. The sky has a greenish-yellow cast to it, and the double suns are very hot. You get the definite impression that it isn't Kansas anymore.

There are broken-down tractors in front, and a long-deserted windmill that hasn't functioned in a long, long time. There are no signs of present habitation.

A dog barks. One can hear the sounds of hens, a rooster crowing, cows mooing and other animals making their own peculiar sounds, but no animal can be seen anywhere.

A lump of something on the ground buzzes with the sound of thousands of horseflies, which seem to swarm closer and closer to you as you move.

The song asks, "How can you keep them down on The Farm, after they've seen Paree?" Well, Paris hasn't changed much, but the Farm sure has. It changes from season to season, and here the seasons change every few minutes.

Notes:

ALICE

Have you ever wondered what it would be like on the other side of the mirror, where everything is backwards and you have to run twice as fast just to stand still? Well, wonder no longer; you'll be in Wonderland in only a moment or two. How long you stay inside out, upside down and backwards is strictly up to you.

The music track in this space was laid down by the rock group called "Ten Mile Spikes".

Notes:

TOWN FOUR

You find yourself in Town Four. There are no other towns. This is a maze of outdoor proportions, and finding your way through it is nothing short of a Miracle.

The wide street smells of sulphur and ammonia fumes; crumpled balls of paper and discarded trash are scattered everywhere. The predominating colors are gray and gray.

It's twilight time, just before the sky darkens into night; a cold wind is blowing, and the trash cans are out on the sidewalks, because here, every night is garbage night.

Notes:

NANA

Every youngster wants to visit Nana. This will cure anyone of that desire.

Notes:

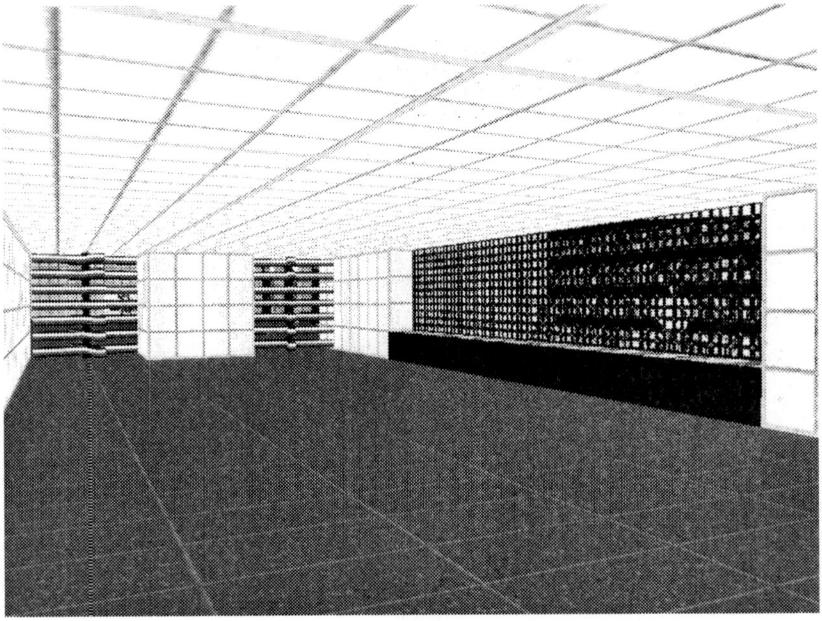

SUBWAY

One finds oneself in a subway; the exit turnstiles are rotating at the end of a platform. Trains start, stop and pass the station. One can hear, but not see, thousands of commuters.

It isn't the people who ride the subway who are the problem; it's the ones who live here.

Notes:

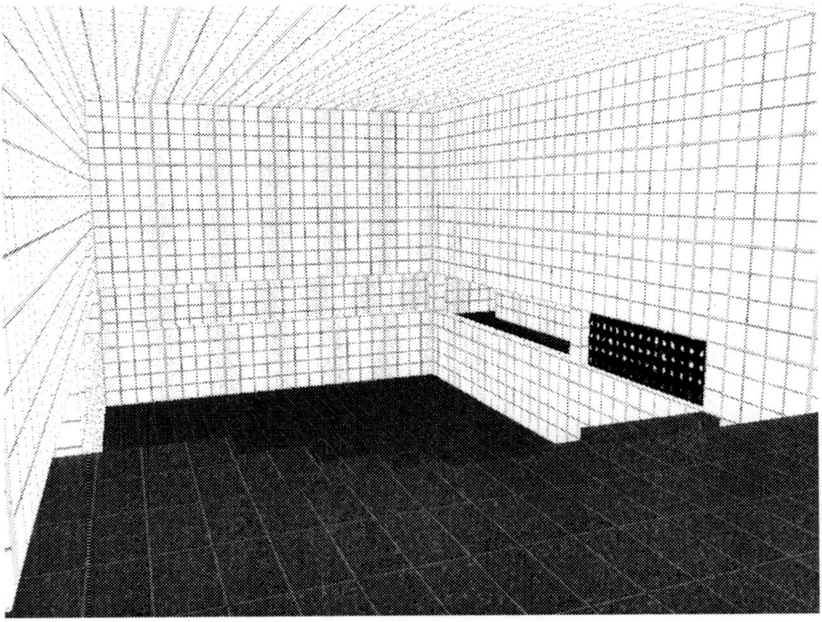

ASTORIA

Rumored to be the largest single underground railway station in the Universe, Astoria is a veritable maze of white ceramic tile, concrete, steel and glass, with an occasional touch of wood; and the third rail is your ultimate bane. Do be careful crossing the tracks, and keep in mind that pretzel vendors who sell food products in subways probably make the things themselves.

Notes:

PARQUET

There is an open door and a hallway beyond a fancy lobby. At the end of the hallway, you can see a set of stairs ascending.

One eventually finds an Art Deco apartment with steps leading down to a sunken living room with oak parquet flooring. The room is slightly rectangular. There are off-white rugs in the living room, a white couch, green lights and surgery lamps shining down from far overhead.

A railing goes around the apartment, behind which is a surrounding balcony in which sits an audience observing the set below, in which you find yourself.

A radio sits on a table. It is dark brown with big dials on it and open light grillwork on the front.

There is a golden ornament around the big dial button.

The radio is playing avant-garde classical music.

The audience reminds one of a medical operating theater. They seem to be taking notes up there.

When one hits the trigger, Levitation takes effect, and one rises through the ceiling.

Notes:

ELEVATED

One finds oneself in an elevated railway station, far above the street. Endless tracks thread through buildings on either side. It is hard to tell which way to go; both directions seem to dim in the distance, and there is no indication that either way leads anywhere in particular.

Notes:

MUSEUM OF NATURAL HISTORY

One finds oneself in a Museum of Natural History. Stuffed animals are everywhere; it is Taxidermy Heaven. There are many exhibits, and if you remain here too long, you will certainly be one of them.

Notes:

MAMA

One wanders from an outside park into a large museum which houses collections of various kinds: meteorites; Egyptian and Mesopotamian antiquities; a Greek collection, and a Roman bath with sculptures and ceramic and glass tile mosaics; a whale exhibit; various wildlife; works of Rembrandt, Van Gogh and other artists, and a variety of gold objects, among other things.

One will discover a restaurant there as well as exhibit halls, and a janitorial area which may or may not offer refuge.

Notes:

LOUVRE

Now one is surrounded by paintings, sculptures, fountains and parklike areas in a single-story art museum. Wandering in here could take hours, days, weeks, months, years, decades and even many centuries. There is no time, only art.

Notes:

ALCHEMY

One finds oneself on the Street of Alchemists; the style of architecture is that of Late Medieval Period, from the 14th to early 20th century. Just East of this area you will find a small version of what you may recognize as Paris Park.

There are iron-grill gates between some of the houses on several blocks of tenements. It is obvious that some sort of disaster has occurred in the recent past, and that no law-enforcement is currently active.

Food, weapons and slave-labor are objects of plunder and corruption; each household is forced to defend itself against raiding parties from other neighborhoods and other lands.

Gangs of former police, armies and neighborhoods wander freely, and a sniper battle rages continually between inhabitants of various buildings in the War Zone just to the East of the Street of Alchemists.

Your task is to find your way through the Alchemical Process, which may take you from house to house and from street to street, discovering in a labyrinthine tangle those keys necessary to open the doors which are, upon arrival in this sector, closed to you.

Notes:

BIKE

It is here that one finds oneself in a tall red brick building, one of many such buildings in the area; there are parks, bike rooms, underground garages beneath the parks, and to the West, slums and tenement houses, warehouses and other less savory areas.

To the South of the Spawning Point, one will find the Eagle Pencil Factory warehouse, a river park and a tunnel leading to a nearby island.

To the North, an elevated railway, the Bijou Theatre, a White Castle Burger Stand and a storefront temple, among other intriguing shops. There are upstairs areas to be explored, and a tiny carousel that can be ridden.

Notes:

SLUMS

Located to the West of Bike one will find the Slums — an area to be avoided at all costs. However, one will surely Spawn here, and so the Slums are, in point of fact, unavoidable. There is a bus system here, which can carry passengers from the Western Depot to the East Depot, but buses tend to be occupied by a variety of very unsavory characters, most of whom are ready to devour one, rend one limb from limb, attack with bladed weapons and flay one's skin down to raw flesh, and other things, far worse.

Within the Slums, one can find fresh laundry, shoes — which seem to be a problem almost anywhere in the Bardo — strong garlic-flavored foods, and of course, sex and drugs, which are almost as available as they would be in prisons.

Somewhere in the Slums, you will encounter the Supermarket, filled with unmovable items on shelves everywhere. There are bargains in the meat department, as you might well imagine. You'll want to avoid complications in the frozen food section, butcher's locker and, of course, the magazine and tabloids at the checkout stands.

Notes:

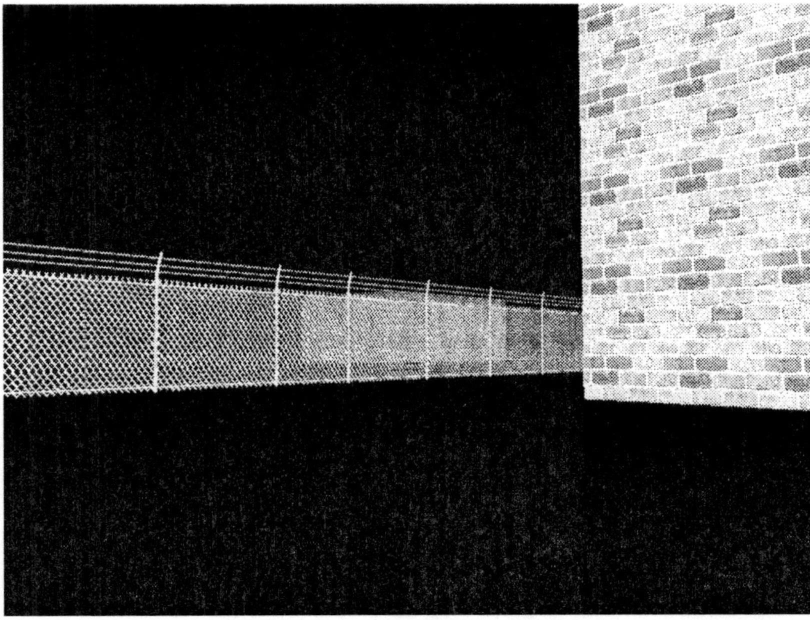

EAGLE PENCIL FACTORY

Located just behind the Eagle Pencil Warehouse, but accessible only through the Slums, the Eagle Pencil Factory is a giant, sprawling manufacturing metropolis in its own right; surrounded by chain link fence and showing only blank red brick walls, it spews out billions of graphite pencils every night.

The smell of hot vulcanized rubber, wood pulp and burning oil dominate the pencil plant.

Notes:

DOCKS

At the far end of the Eagle Pencil Factory one finds oneself at the Loading Docks; vicious guard dogs howl and bark, shots ring out continually, and mayhem rules the dark, starless night. A warmish wind blows continually through the electrified chain link fences which surround the Docks. Your goal is to find your way through this maze of low brick buildings to the underground passage which leads to the School.

Notes:

SCHOOL

The School is exactly as you remember it; the classrooms are far too small, the desks too low, the principal is always just around the corner and the lockers are always open.

Notes:

WOODLAND

Camp Woodland is located on a vast hilly area deep in the Resort Mountain Range. Here one will find exactly those things one expects to find at any summer camp — nature trail, waterfall, pool, ping pong, capture the flag, crafts bungalow; everything that all summer camps have in common, except that there are no counselors, no other campers, no food and no letters to and from home, and no escape at the end of summer.

Notes:

ZENA MILL

The Zena Mill was built in 1710; at least, that's what the sign says just at the curve outside the lumbermill. The grist mill and gardener's cottage lie just South, along the largish pond below the triple waterfall. Downstream are farms and other, smaller mills, each one long-abandoned, as is this one.

Further downstream one finds the usual that one has grown to expect in the Lower Bardos: cannibals, ghouls, goblins and the inevitable zombies. The Black Gang roams freely through this area, and can be of some assistance to the unafraid.

Notes:

ANGEL

Now one will Spawn into the Angels of No Mercy Hospital; it is a place of healing, but who cares if a hospital is healed?

Notes:

WARD ISLE

Here one finds help in psychological levels; there are a variety of mental health areas, including Craft Therapy, Saturday Night Social Dances, Shock Therapy, Lithium, Prozac, Nembutal, Seconal, Ice Cold Chill Pools, Cold Sheet Wraps and, of course, if all else fails, Pre-Frontal Lobotomy.

Notes:

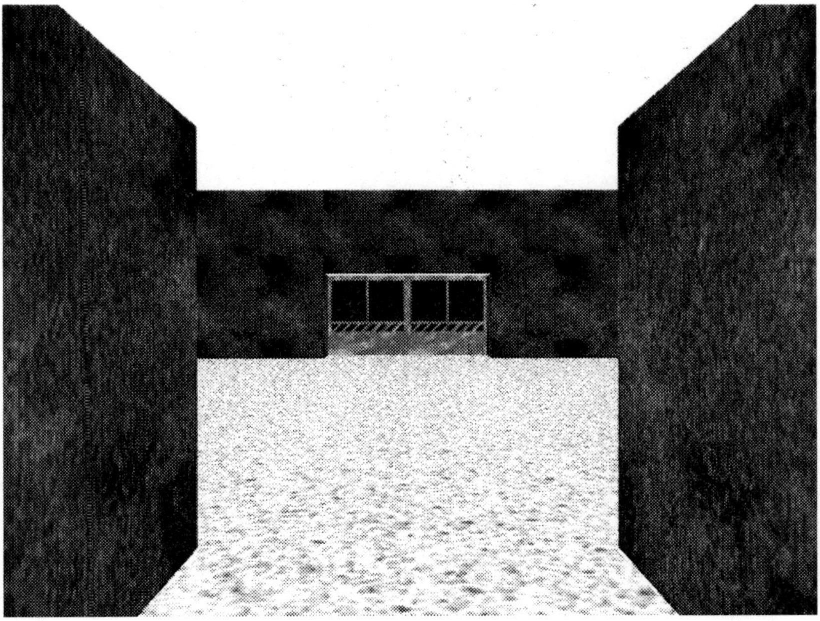

PENTAGON

One finds oneself in a Pentagon-shaped building which reminds one of the military establishment headquarters, yet there are definite and singular differences between the physical level and this one; notably, the Bardo space does not feature zombies as does the corresponding building on the physical plane which was built from this higher vision.

Notes:

ARMY HOSPITAL

A series of long, low buildings, punctuated by tall, wide medical areas. Here, one can enjoy the healing power of restless slumber and interminable periods between mealtimes; nurses and orderlies seem to be nearby, but are never around when you need them. Somewhere in all this white antiseptic atmosphere one will find the exit to Glendale.

Notes:

GLENDALE

Not quite a Glen, not quite a Dale, this mighty suburb of low buildings is home to the Bardo Cemetery, after which the Glendale Forest Lawn Cemetery was fashioned; to the North, one can find what seems to be a candle shop amid many small suburban homes; another storefront in this otherwise very residential neighborhood is a black-walled building that at first glance seems to be your ordinary everyday Alchemist's shop, but which definitely calls for more exploration.

In a palm tree-surrounded grassy lawn just outside the Alchemist's shop, one will note a levitating Alchemist near a green chalkboard, upon which is written a series of subjects to be studied by someone or something, noting the date for a Final Exam.

Notes:

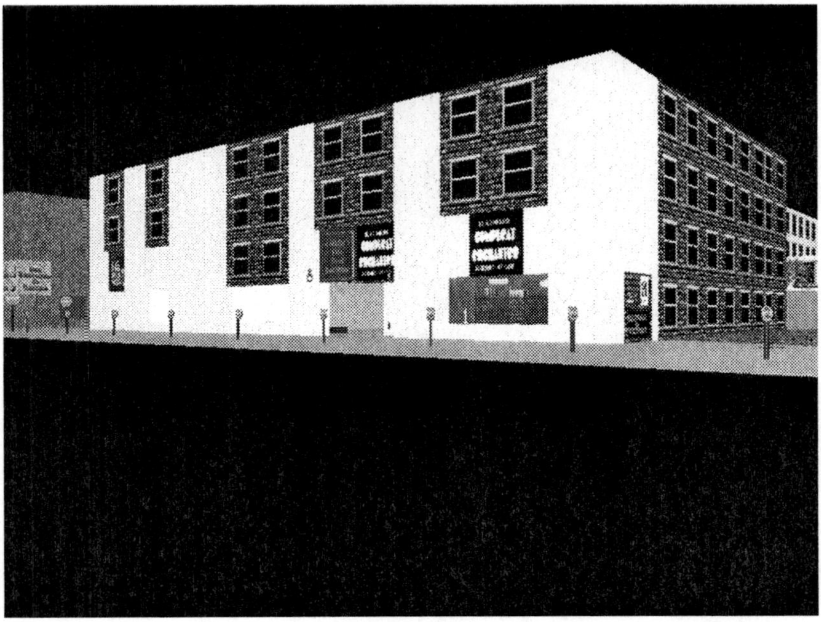

OTHEREND

Here one finds oneself at what is definitely the Wrong End of a popular shopping district, a wide boulevard running East and West; again one can find an Alchemist's Shop, slightly different from the one in the Glendale zone. There is also a Taxi Shop, a shortened form of Taxidermist's Shop. One will also find a glass shop, a Hippie Head Shop, a Mystical Temple and a variety of other shops.

Slightly to the South, on a gentle upward slope, one will discover a private home which houses many items of interest.

There are some areas which are blocked; obstacles can be overcome.

Notes:

OTIS

One will Spawn into what might or might not be some sort of school; cold white stucco buildings surround a parking lot. There are what may or may not be classrooms, but no teachers, no students, no faculty advisors, no admin. Just you and an empty building.

Notes:

OTIS LIBRARY

A large library, otherwise known as the Akashic Library.

There is a huge board with lighted numbers. You find yourself at an enormous counter, where you are told to take a ticket, that your number will eventually be called.

Nearby, one can find a vending machine similar to a copier, which issues what are called "Sanity Certificates", available for One Coin of unspecified value.

Without this certificate, one cannot expect to get anywhere in this realm.

One can find one's way eventually through the Security Gate into the stacks, if one is not obsessed about security.

One can go downstairs, where there are more stacks.

Even further down another flight of stairs one can find the Men's Room and Ladies' Room, each of which leads to the appropriate rebirth sexuality.

One can find another way, which leads down a long hallway.

Without a library card, no books can be removed, but who would want to take something out of this place, anyway?

Notes:

NORTON

"Oh, no, not this again! Here we are again. Please help me," you moan.

"Help you what?" comes the answer.

You are in a small apartment. You can run, you can hide, you can go elsewhere. But there is No Escape.

Time stops. You feel faint, waiting for Time to start again. By changing the pointers on the clock, you are able to start time, but it requires constant maintenance, and you find yourself unable to maintain.

On the TV set, an ongoing display of horrifying, unending mortal combat.

In the kitchen, blue food is served.

In the bathroom, an electric bath is waiting to suck you in and keep you there.

On the bookshelves, books are waiting for you to fall into them and become them.

Everywhere there are traps, lifetimes to be lived, each object calling you to become them, to live their lives, to identify with them, to fall into sleep, sleep, deep, deep slumber, to forget who and what you are, to sleep, perchance to dream.

Notes:

GEMINI

One arrives at what might be described as a Thieves' Market, a black-walled indoor mall with a variety of small shopping booths; one will find a music shop, a poster shop, blacklight items, a tiny "Head Shop", clothing for the very hip, strange music-reactive lights, lava lamps and all manner of strange items, as well as the inevitable Alchemist's Shop just near the outer door.

Deep below the street level, in the sub-basement, one will find a stage filled with amps and instruments, a place of surrealistic underground music.

Outside, one will discover a Mexican restaurant, G.I. Surplus store, Wax Museum and a variety of dining establishments including a steak house and an Italian spaghetti kitchen. On diagonally opposite corners, the Gold Cup, which is the local "meatrack" which features male and female hookers standing outside waiting for pickups, and George's Burgers, where most of the merchants eat their hurried meals.

Your task, should you decide to accept it, is to thread your way through all this misery and suffering, finding your way to the Ultimate Goal, which is, in this case, the Freeway.

Notes:

FREEWAY

One thing that every driver discovers about Freeways is that none of them are actually free.

Notes:

FANTASIA

You awaken from a long, deep dreamless sleep to discover yourself in a large theater in which nothing is playing.

The screen is brilliant with plain white light, yet the audience reacts with laughter, tears and other strong lower emotional manifestations, obviously projecting their own images onto the empty screen.

One is aware that the audience is watching some invisible action onscreen and acting it out, taking part in the filming of this multiplicity of lifetime dramas, at one and the same time.

With a great effort, one is able to pull back away from the invisible Life Story Fantasy Film before one is drawn into it once again, leading to lethargic sleep and a long, deep blackout into Tripping.

The walk toward the back of the theater seems impossibly slow; the slight ramp should not be as difficult as it seems, and yet, you are barely crawling as you exit the theater. It almost seems as if the empty screen is exerting a powerful magnetic pull, drawing you back into your seat.

The lobby of the theater has obviously seen better days. It is decorated in late 19th century ornate style, with an overabundance of gold-leaf and plush carpeting.

Upstairs one can find a balcony, and a washroom, if a toilet seems necessary in this situation; it seems to be a unisex convenience, filled with a combination of open commodes and urinals. The floor is literally flooded with a deep pool of urine, which reeks with age.

Elaborate crystal chandeliers hang from the high ceiling; one can hear, and sometimes see, large, red-eyed rats scampering about, scurrying into and out of holes in the floor, walls and furnishings.

The stairway has no rail, and it is easy to fall to the thickly carpeted floor below. The atmosphere is hotly close, musty and overwhelmingly heavy.

Notes:

MMM

You are now in the Triple M, the Magical Mystery Museum. It is as it sounds; full of magic and mystery. You will find here the Secret Key to the I-Ching, and a really interesting display of mummies, as well as a very reasonably priced gift shop, if you're in the market for a gift shop.

Deities abound, and tour guides will be happy to show you The Way, if a guide can, indeed, be found; yet the whole place seems to have been abandoned, perhaps quite recently. The fact is that everyone left the moment they heard that you had arrived.

Notes:

HOLYWOOD

Hooray for Holywood, that's what they say. You may enjoy the Star Walk, where the sidewalk is littered with memorials to the stage, screen and recording stars of Yesteryear. You'll find your own name inscribed somewhere along the route, but that's not important now.

Notes:

COSMO 01

One finds oneself on a cold, empty street, with many attractions and distractions. There is a strong, bitterly cold wind blowing at all times, from West to East, so powerful that one must lean into it in order to move against it.

Fighting the wind, one can travel along the deserted streets and boulevards. The low buildings have the strange effect of being nothing but flat, fake movie fronts with no substance and no depth.

There is a warm comfortable restaurant somewhere nearby, where one can sit at a table or counter and enjoy hot coffee or tea, and partake of hot dogs, hamburgers and french fries, or a delicious meal of raw tuna and woodborer worms.

Eventually one may find one's way to a building called Cosmo.

Here, one discovers a marble chamber in which geometric patterns of light and dark are described on the floor, and gold and red paint appear on the ceiling, in the manner copied by the ancient Egyptians.

There is a slight echo in this chamber. There is an old-fashioned elevator to the left of the entrance, and a tiny shop of some kind. There is a long stairway on the far side to the left, leading upward into unguessable heights.

Notes:

COSMO OFFICE

On the Third Floor of Cosmo, one can find bathrooms for one and all; down the hall one discovers a timeless classroom. The floor of the classroom is carpeted in thick, plush champagne-pink wool. The walls are white and schoolroom desk-chairs are placed within. The lighting is soft, glowing with a peachy hue.

In another, deeper chamber, walls are draped with soft white, almost fleshy, fabric; a double-cubed boxlike altar stands at the far end, backed with a strange, yet somehow familar, oriental carpet.

Ten large copper disks inscribed with odd geometric calligraphic designs are placed in a pattern of the Sepher Sephiroth, the Tree of Life, upon the thickly carpeted floor.

Clouds of heavy incense fill the room. Suddenly there is a lurch, as if the entire universe had shifted a fraction of an inch.

One can now leave the chamber, outside which the corridor has now become enormous; one floats down the passageway toward an impossibly large chamber within which unimaginable things are happening.

In the central chamber are giant slug-like creatures, perhaps millions of miles away, yet within easy sight; everything is enormous here, except you.

Doors yawn, beckoning you to fall into them. The Giant Central Chamber opens to you, daring you to fall into it, drawing you down just as a canyon or a high building makes you fear that you might have a sudden urge to jump.

Your goal is to find the Traveler's Aid Station before you are drawn into the Main Chamber of Grand Central Station.

Notes:

COSMO ALLEY

Now that you have found your way through Grand Central and are no longer a slug, you can pick a path down Cosmo Alley, where every good turn deserves another, and no good deed goes unpunished.

Notes:

BLOOD ALLEY

One arrives in Blood Alley, where a party is ongoing somewhere nearby and cars can be heard crashing; screams of victims occasionally pierce the air. A river of blood flows down the mountainside.

One Spawns within the basement of a strange mountain cabin, perhaps a small ski resort. There is a kitchen and main room on the ground floor, and upstairs one will find several guestrooms and a bathroom.

Outside, a porch and a small temple below, near Blood Stream.

Somewhere, a road lies before one, leading to a mountain mall in which one will discover the Phantom Bookstore, Kung Fu Natural Food Restaurant, Bob's Pizza Hut, Infinity Videoshop and many other delights of the senses.

Downstairs in the largish mountain resort mall, one will find Rachel's Health Spa, Lizardo's Colonics Clinic, The Busy

Businessperson's Fast Foods Lunch Counter, Mom & Pop's Szechuan Take-out, QuickestCopy and Jack's Internet Cafe, as well as a small Bardo Training Center for those who missed it during their lifetime.

Notes:

BUCK'S BOOKS

Just down the street from the Mountain Mall, one will encounter Buck's Books, specializing in antiquarian books, mostly occult, supernatural and mystical, with an occasional Book of Shadows and a history of economics or comic book apocrypha.

An overpowering musty smell permeates the close stillness of the interior of the shop, which is deep and narrow, seeming to extend into infinity.

Somewhere in here, one will find what one needs to pass through this space; probably it will envision itself in the form of the *American Book of the Dead*.

The gaslit interior flickers slightly. A white cat inhabits the deepest realm of the oversized green-leather Morris chair where the bookseller might have been.

There are heavy layers of thick dust everywhere; moths abound, and cobwebs seem to have been spun in every available corner. A tinny, scratchy recording of classical music plays somewhere, and the atmosphere is elusive at best.

Leatherbound and vellum-covered ancient books are everywhere; it is here that you will find the *Handbook for the Recently Deceased*, *Handbook for the Incredulous*, *Handbook for the Perpetually Overwhelmed* as well as the one for which you are looking, if you can keep your attention on the goal at hand.

Notes:

REFINERY

If you've ever wondered what goes on in one of those oil refineries, this is not the time to find out. A cold, bitter wind whips through, biting into the very soul. Black starless sky, emptiness and quietude. Nothing here but misery and pain, yet somewhere there is a key, and you must find it.

Notes:

QUACK

A series of strange, mindless spaces each leading from nowhere to nowhere, yet in the end, nothing.

Notes:

PLAYPEN

As we near rebirth, a Giant Playpen For The Very Small.

Notes:

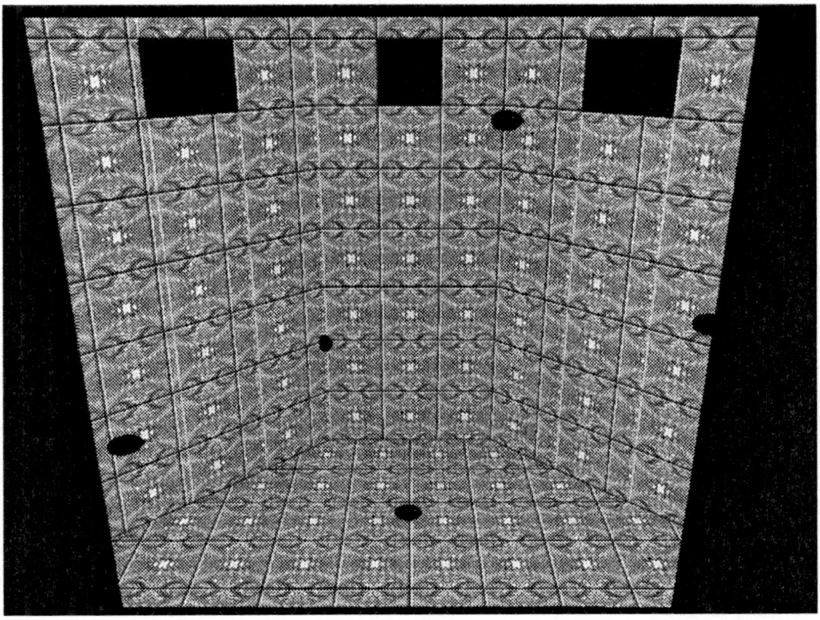

GRAND CENTRAL

From Grand Central, all things are possible, yet Grand Central Station of the Bardos will Prevail. If you ever had thoughts of going rather rapidly through the Lower Bardo, you're in for a big disappointment.

Notes:

GRAND HOTEL

The Grand Hotel lives up to its name, at least the "Hotel" part. It is a place of meetings, of pairing, of Love and Romantic Entanglements, of mating and sweating and moaning and groaning, of humping and bumping and panting and groping. It is a place that leads only toward rebirth.

Notes:

BAKERY

Need a crumpet, a bagel or a baguette? You'll knead some dough to get your fill, but at The Bakery, you've definitely come to the right place. Ah, the aroma of baking bread! Cookies and Cake! Torts and Truffles! By the time you have come to this place, Rebirth is inevitable, the Open Womb lies ahead, and here, in the womb, you are Baked In The Oven Until Done.

Notes:

DEAD CLAY

Ready for Rebirth? Here you come, ready or not!

Notes:

CRUSHER

You are drawn into Rebirth through the Crusher, smashed down into the Birth Canal, ready for Delivery by the fastest route! Neither snow, nor sleet, nor gloom of night will keep this courier from his appointed rounds!

Notes:

BARDOTOWN OVERWORLD

A mapping recap of all that you have experienced; one last Bardo Dream before awakening in a brand-new body! Welcome Home! Waaaaahhhhhh!

Index of Bardo Stations

General Index

Symbols

A

B

E

F

G

H

I

J

K

L

M

N

O

P

Q

R

S

T

U

V

W

Y

Z